SOVIET
ART AND ARTISTS

by

JACK CHEN

THE PILOT PRESS LTD.
LONDON, W.C.1

*First published September, 1944,
by the Pilot Press, Ltd., 45, Great
Russell Street, London, W.C.1.*

ACKNOWLEDGMENTS

I express my thanks to the editors of *The Studio* and *Art and Industry* for kind permission to reprint material contributed to the special Soviet numbers of their journals.

J. C.

Printed in Great Britain by The Chiswick Press,
New Southgate, London, N.11.

CONTENTS

*

LIST OF ILLUSTRATIONS

★

I

THE ROLE OF ART THROUGH SOVIET EYES.

Art belongs to the people, its roots should penetrate deeply into the very thick of the masses of the people. It should be comprehensible to these masses and loved by them. It should unite the emotions, thoughts and will of these masses and arouse them.

LENIN.

★

THE FIRST time I met a Russian Bolshevik was in China, 1926. He was Michael Borodin, Russian adviser to Sun Yat-sen, the man who was reputed at that time to be the "brains behind the Chinese revolution". We naturally talked about art for I had just started drawing cartoons for the Press. Borodin however could not resist switching the conversation to the arts that he most delighted in—opera and music. He told us of the time when as a student in Moscow he would wait for a whole day in the queue to get a seat up "in the Gods" to hear Chaliapin sing. The rich Muscovites had literally bought up all the best seats in the theatre. Seats indeed were almost hereditary. The names of the owners were stamped on their backs.

"Now anyone can go to the Opera", said Borodin. "The Soviets have given art back to the people. . . . Peasants and workers sit in the Tsar's box!"

Borodin was a persuasive propagandist both for the Soviet Union and Opera. It was only a year or so later that I arrived in Red Moscow to get a closer view of this new society and sat—or rather stood, for it was crowded out—in the Tsar's box myself to see "Lohengrin" in a production more magnificent than the Tsar's.

It was here in Moscow that as a student and artist I came to appreciate the common sense view of art of the Bolsheviks. It was here that I learned that the Soviet Communist is a practical humanist, and that it is from this standpoint that he looks upon art. He sees art as a special form of social communion, as a means whereby feelings, emotions and thoughts can be communicated from one or more people—the artists—to others in a particularly intense, pleasurable and effective way. At its best, art educates man in the highest ideals and qualities of emotion. And then it is highly entertaining. At its worst, it descends to the depths of pornographic or political bestiality where it ceases to be art. All art, in this sense is "propaganda" for good or bad. Usually however the term "propaganda" is used to describe those special forms of art which are more openly and avowedly publicistic and rely for their effect on more flamboyant and direct means of quickly "putting across" their point. Thus good or effective propaganda may be good art. Good art is not necessarily good or effective propaganda.

The Soviet artist too makes his distinction between the *Fine Arts:* music, plays, poems, pictures, etc., and the *Applied Arts*. Pots and pans, chairs and clothes, can have "artistic significance". Made by the hands of an artist or good artisan their practical function can be enhanced by heightening the degree of their aesthetic significance, but the essential social role of the fine arts is ideological. Their function is to organise and influence man's *psyche*—the sum total of man's spiritual life—his thoughts and feelings, his consciousness and sub-consciousness—through the medium of his senses. The essential function of a picture, is to communicate certain feelings, emotions and ideas by means of its imagery, and thus affect or stimulate a new cycle of human activity. Art can only be fully understood as a social phenomenon.

The skilful artist thus wields an extraordinary and subtle power. He can inspire his audience with heroic humanism in the vein of a Michelangelo, fill them with abounding human sympathy in the vein of a Rembrandt òr lead them to frivolity in the style of Boucher or Fragonard. Like Daumier, the great bourgeois republican, he can help to build up the understanding and confidence of a class struggling for progressive human ideals, or like Matisse, he may merely register and encourage the relaxation of that same class into hedonistic enjoyment.

Where does the concept of "beauty" enter into this Soviet

estimation of the social role of art? It lies at the heart of the problem. The works of Michelangelo, Rembrandt, Boucher, Daumier and Matisse, for all their great variety and antagonistic ideals, have all, at one time or another, been well nigh universally acclaimed as being beautiful. In turn, they have been decried at various times and by various groups and classes, as being repulsive. The nudes of Michelangelo in the Sixtine were given painted clothes. Rembrandt had a spectacular fall from popularity and was abused for having "merely achieved an effect of rotten-ness". Boucher, to the Puritans, was the artist of the libertines, and so on. Yet the cultured man of to-day can appreciate all these artists and many more just as varied. It is clear that these artists express very different concepts of beauty, concepts that in some cases are mutually exclusive. Beauty, then, is not an inherent quality of a work of art. It is a relation set up between the viewer and the work of art, though naturally the work of art must have qualities of form and content capable of evoking an aesthetic response. But what is this aesthetic response or sense of the beautiful?

Some of the ultra-left intellectuals in the early days of the Soviets denied the very existence of aesthetic sensibility or of beauty. These concepts were denounced as bourgeois myths, part of an upper class conspiracy to preserve the exclusiveness of art by surrounding it with an aura of mysticism and a barrage of highbrow talk about "inspiration", "eternal beauty" and whatnot. It is true that much bourgeois art criticism has tended to prevent a common-sense approach to art. In both club and pub, opinions on politics or religion are offered without introduction, but opinions on art are almost invariably prefixed with "Of course I don't know anything about art, but . . .". Nevertheless as a Chinese writer has it: "If the wicked eat rice, that is no reason why the good shouldn't eat it."

Plekhanov, one of the first of the Russian Marxists to deal with questions of aesthetics, quotes a passage from Darwin in which the scientist refers to: " . . . the pleasure given by certain colours, forms and sounds which may fairly be called a sense of the beautiful (which) appears in both men and animals, but with cultivated men, such sensations are, however, intimately associated with complex ideas and trains of thought...". "Obviously," adds Darwin, "no animal would be capable of admiring such scenes as the heavens at night, a beautiful landscape, or refined music; such such high tastes are acquired through culture, and depend on complex associations..." Plekhanov and the most representative contemporary Soviet writers on art, infer that, as Darwin suggests, man has developed the faculties necessary for aesthetic appreciation as a product of biological evolution, but that, as Darwin again indicates by the use of the phrase "cultivated man", it is *social conditions* that determine exactly which "complex ideas and trains of thought" are evoked by a particular work of art or natural object. In other words, man's biological nature is such that he can have aesthetic tastes, but it is the conditions of his economic and social life that determine how this possibility is translated into a reality, it is these social conditions that determine why it is that a member of a particular society or of a certain class or group in that society has particular aesthetic tastes and not others. Thus man's understanding of beauty and the whole problem of aesthetics is brought into conformity with the general principles of historical materialism. Since (as Marx, Engels, Plekhanov, Lenin and Stalin and others have shown), the conditions of man's existence are determined in their turn by the prevailing method of social-economic production, it is easy to understand how it is that different societies, or different classes within a particular form of society, have different and even mutually exclusive understandings or conceptions of beauty. It is natural that the early hunting tribes should have taken their pictorial motifs from the animal world, though they were constantly surrounded by an abundance of flowers and shrubs. It is no less comprehensible that the denizens of the European metropolises should see in flowers a splendid and fragile beauty. Then take the peasant whose ideal of feminine beauty is a buxom country wench with rosy cheeks and healthy thighs, or the aristocratic aesthete whose ideal of womanhood is slim and fragile. And it becomes just as understandable why the progressive and rising class of the burghers in Florence should have hailed the virile genius of Michelangelo, while their economic descendants in the France that produced Vichy should have been perfervid admirers of Matisse with his odalisques and decorative arabesques of colour.

Michelangelo's paintings and sculpture were part of the progressive, dynamic and realist ideological "superstructure" or way of thought of the upsurging burghers and merchant princes of Florence. They embodied the spirit of the Renaissance. As the artistic representative of these progressive classes, Michelangelo gave confidence and a renewal of spiritual energy to them. And Michelangelo was not alone. In painting he was but one of a whole pleiad of masters ministering to the same end. Sculpture, architecture, music, literature, skilled artisans in stone and metal work all took part in the work of "putting over the ideas" of the burghers, their democracy, their realism; at the same time these artists were contradicting and battling down the hostile ideas and feelings of those feudal classes and their hangers-on who clung to and defended the old order of things. A vast mass of artistic creation went into the making of the glorious Renaissance. We still feel its influence to-day.

And Matisse, and the frippery of the Jardin des Modes, Jean Cocteau, and the vibrating luxury of the vast *Normandie*, the Folies Bergére—this was the ideological accompaniment of the fall of bourgois France.

The artists' work consciously or unconsciously builds up or debases the mentality of his class and weaves those complex associations of thoughts and feelings that the admirers of his work call "beauty."

The Soviet Communists thus take an exalted view of the tremendous power and scope of art. Accepting all the implications of this view, they early set about exploring ways and means of applying art to the task of building the new socialist, and further Communist, society, and of helping to create the improved type of man, ideologically fitted to build and live in such a co-operative society.

Russian Communist artists and statesmen before the Revolution of 1917 faced up to the task of mobilising art on the side of history and progress, just as the great leaders of the past had done for their times. "Art should unite the emotions, thoughts and will of the masses and arouse them", wrote Lenin. When their party achieved state leadership, they set about making use of all the resources of the state for the advancement of socialism, putting all art and culture at the disposal of the people, to enable art to be universally enjoyed and thus achieve universal culture.

In the years before the October Revolution, when the Bolshevik majority of the Russian Social-Democratic Party (the present Communist Party) was still a hunted and persecuted group, it did succeed in winning over many of the students and artist intellectuals. The literary criticisms of Plekhanov, Lenin's profound exposition of his philosophic ideas, Lunarcharsky's brilliant art commentaries, were storm centres of discussion among Russian intellectuals. They rallied the arts and artists to the side of the revolutionary forces led by the Russian working class and its political party.

They helped to educate and influence the efforts of such men as Gorky, Mayakovsky, Eisenstein, Pudovkin, cartoonists and poster artists such as Moor and Deni, and Yefimov. In the battle for the October Revolution such widely diversified groups as Futurists, Constructivists, Symbolists, Suprematists aided in the attack on Tsarism. In the hungry heroic days of the Civil War and Intervention, the Soviet government expressed its high estimation of the value of art and artists by the practical method of giving them extra food rations. Those hungry days saw an unexampled renaissance of the Russian Theatre. Ragged, sitting in their coats and felt boots for warmth, Moscow audiences revelled in masterpieces of theatrical art at the Moscow Art Theatre, the Vakhtangov, the Theatre of the Revolution, the Meyerhold, and then entrained for the battle fronts. New poems were printed in books made of wrapping paper. The sculptors were invited by Lenin to take over the city squares and create monumental propaganda for the new society. Mayakovsky declaimed his poems to audiences at the "people's university" in the Moscow Polytechnic Museum, and then went in to battle for his artistic principles with his fists against enraged representatives of the old traditions. When he recited at the "Lodge Café", a hangout of the anarchists, his supporters—workers of the Red Guard—held their revolvers at the ready.

Splendid revolutionary posters shouted their message from bullet-spattered walls. One morning a "symphony" of factory whistles deafened the Moscow air. Tatlin designed a revolving monument to the Third International. Those were exciting days in the art world. Art came out of the ivory tower with a vengeance, and strode the streets among the people. These extravagant manifestations of revolutionary art were talked about, discussed, criticised. There was more than enough solid achievement however to prevent them from being merely dismissed as nine-day sensations. Eisenstein's "Battleship Potemkin" is still the unrivalled masterpiece of the screen, Mayakovsky is to-day hailed as the "best, the most talented poet of our epoch" (Stalin), Vakhtangov's fantasy "Princess Turandot" won world-wide acclaim ten years later as winner of the International Theatre Festival in bourgeois Paris. Perhaps the manifestations of public interest in art have since been less flamboyant and explosive, but in the succeeding years of the Soviet Union, art has none the less steadily deepened and spread throughout the land and the people and its achievements have been far reaching and important.

Animated by the democratic driving power of the Russian Communists and Soviet life, art cannot possibly be regarded as a "museum piece", as a source of financial speculation, as a prerogative of the wealthy few or a private playground of the intelligentsia. There are no wealthy few, there is no "coterie" of intellectuals in the Soviet Union. Speculation in picture-buying just as speculative trading in any other public good, is a criminal offence. With the consolidation of the Soviet system and the ending of private property in the means of production, with the building up of a great socialist state industry and trading system, a socialist agriculture and an all-pervasive co-operative economy, the whole basis of art has changed. The artist has lost the doubtful favours of the rare, rich patron and the more than doubtful services of the artists' agent, but he has gained most solid grounds for a vast development of the arts through having a vastly ex-

panded market for his productions—a market in which he is at
liberty to "trade"—and a vastly securer social position as a result
of the efforts of his own Trade Union and Co-operative organisations and the sedulous care of the state.

Lenin, founder of the Soviet state, was sparing of his opinions
on those art questions which he felt needed the knowledge of the
expert, but he did not hesitate to expound with great vigour his
opinions and policies on general questions of art. As a progressive and democratic statesman-philosopher, Lenin argued,
as the quotation heading this chapter shows, that to be fully
effective as a human "good", as a progressive force, art must be
closely woven into the life of every individual citizen so as to
broaden and enrich his whole personality. The Soviet statesman
is thus vitally interested in the task of making art truly democratic alike in form, content and distribution. Art takes on a new
and unprecedented importance for state and society. The responsibility of the artist increases and society develops a new respect
for him. He is no longer regarded as "an eccentric" or a "hired
entertainer". He is an "architect of the social soul", a chief
sourse of enlightened human enjoyment. Expressing this new
attitude to art, Soviet museums and exhibitions have been made
specially attractive to the public, art has been shorn of anything
that suggests snobbery or exclusiveness, and numerous organisations have been formed for the free and widespread distribution
of art and artistic creation. Trade Unions, local Soviets, collective
farms, the Red Army and Navy, all have special committees to
arrange art shows, art education and the fostering of artistic
talent. The artists themselves have created their own clubs,
unions and co-operatives to organise their relations with this vast
new audience and "clientele". Art becomes as much a necessity
of life as municipal lighting or elementary education. The artist
becomes as indispensable a member of society as any other
teacher of essential knowledge. Art, for the first time has the
chance of being really "individual", for it becomes really accessible to every individual. It can shed the spurious "individuality"
that in western society is only another name for "exclusiveness".

The size of the enormous audience that the new art policy has created can be gauged from the fact that in the Soviet Union in 1940-41, 80,000,000 people attended performances in the 850 theatres; 44,500,000 people attended concerts of symphonic and chamber music. In the four years from 1936 to 1940, 5,000 different books on art were published in editions totalling 32,542,000 copies. In 1940 alone, 1,338 different titles on art were published with a total edition of 7,534,000 copies. The U.S.S.R. is the greatest book publishing country in the world.

The state budget for art in 1941 was 1,700,000,000 Rs. 780,000,000 Rs. of this was provided by the Government, the remainder was scheduled to come from the receipts of the State theatres, cinemas and other enterprises. 95,000,000 Rs. were earmarked for the organisation of exhibitions, art festivals and art scholarships. And this latter sum does not include the valuable annual Stalin Prizes for art, which carry the title of Laureate and grants of from 10,000 to 100,000 Rs.

But the artist is not only the teacher of society. He is the decorator, the adorner of the peoples' life. No October Anniversary, Red Army Day, Youth Day, May Day or other great public festival or pageant is complete without new songs, new symphonies, new poems, plays, films, murals, banners, animated cartoons and carnival processions designed and composed by leading artists.

At the height of the siege of Leningrad, on the day that Von Leeb gave the order "Leningrad must be captured at all costs!" and hurled his armoured divisions at the city's defences, the Soviet composer Shostakovich announced at his A.R.P. post: "I am completing my Seventh Symphony in honour of the coming Anniversary of the October Revolution and Soviet victory!" The Leningrad City Soviet announced prizes for the best October song. The composer Asafyev sat down to his piano in his coat and fur cap in a fireless room. The city's artists began preparing banners and cartoons for the great festival day, their rifles lying ready by the drawing tables. They remembered the words of the hero in the fascist Hans Johst's play: "When I hear the word culture, I reach for my revolver!"

Von Leeb, frustrated and beaten, has relapsed into the obscurity of ignominy. Leningrad has been freed and has seen the destruction of its enemies. Shostakovich's symphony remains as a memorial to the unconquerable spirit of man.

BEFORE THE END

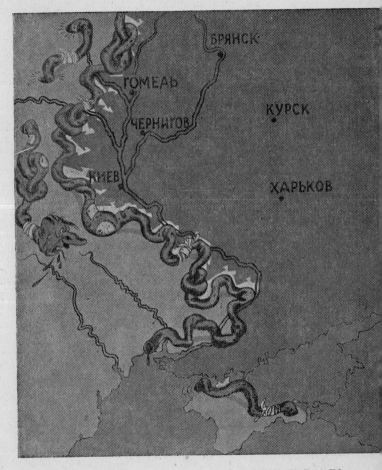

Cartoon by Boris Efinov.

"German front line after straightening."

II

THE ARTIST'S TRAINING

A follower of Lenin cannot be just a specialist in his favourite science or art; he must also be a social and political worker taking a vital interest in the destinies of his country. He must be well acquainted with the laws of social development; he must be able to apply these laws and must actively participate in the political guidance of the country.

J. V. STALIN

at the 18th Congress of the
All-Union Communist Party.

*

I ARRIVED in Moscow in the autumn of 1927. The New Economic Policy that followed the period of emergency War Communism, had almost completely rehabilitated the economic life of the country, which had been all but ruined by the civil war and intervention. Industry and agriculture had regained their 1914 level. The world was waiting to see whither Russia would now go. Under Stalin's leadership the Soviets announced the Five-Year Plan. The figures of factories to be built and lands to be tilled seemed fantastic for such an apparently exhausted country. Those "in the know" in London, Paris, Washington and Berlin laughed. But the "Reds" went ahead. In record time they transformed the country from a backward agrarian state into one of the foremost industrial powers of the world.

But in 1927 the triumphs of socialist construction were yet to come. Most of the Moscow streets were still cobble-stoned. Taxis were a rarity. Even the Foreign Affairs Commissariat only boasted a couple of ancient Rolls-Royces, and the battered *droshkys* took full advantage of the last days of "private enterprise" by charging exorbitant fares for the shortest of journeys. The fashionable dress for men was the Russian blouse, leather cap and short leather coat that had been more or less the uniform of the famous political commissars during the revolution and civil war. But the only man I ever saw in a red blouse was an Englishman. The flamboyant attire of the Nepmen and their women contrasted shrilly with the general dowdiness of a country that had only just succeeded in setting its clothing-mills in operation again. As in all agricultural countries the people were sublimely unpunctual, and a meeting that began only a half hour late was considered "on time." Curious foreign tourists and "special correspondents" arrived armed with "flit" guns and toilet paper, "did" the country, and, returning to civilisation, announced with all the aplomb of a Columbus that "none of the lavatories in Russia works" and that the Metropol hotel was infested with bugs. To the vast majority of the Western peoples Russia was "an Asiatic country."

It was quite true that there were bugs in Russia's best hotel. I know. I was bitten by them. Russia's millions of peasants had not yet learned to use water closets, but these facts were only sidelights on the news. The real truth, the salient fact was that in their unorthodox way the Russians had cleared the economic and political ground for one of the most vast social changes that the world has seen . . . the building of a classless society. They had indeed already laid the foundations for that new society and the groundwork of a splendid educational system in which art, so long a Cinderella in the modern world, was at last getting a fair share of attention.

But, many things seemed very unorthodox in those days of 1927. For instance, my entry into the university.

Before my arrival in Moscow I had had no special art training, but I had drawn many cartoons for the Chinese press during the great days of the 1924-27 Northern Expedition of the Republicans. Finding myself in Moscow, I decided to get some fundamental art training at the VKhUTEMAS[1] as the Higher Art and Technical Workshops were called. I spoke no Russian in those days, so a friend took me along to the School with my scrap book of cartoons. In those days the Director of the school was Pavel Novit-

----
[1] Vishe KhUdozhestvenny TEKhnicheskoy MASterskoy.

sky—ugly, shock-headed and brilliant theoretician of the ultra-left "October" group. He glanced through my pictures, said shortly "Khorosho!"[1] and the interview concluded. I became a Moscow art student. It was as simple as that.

Actually, I found that very many students had been enrolled in this seemingly unorthodox way. One, Vanya, had been a farm lad whose sketches had been noticed by the local Soviet Chairman. They had sent him to Moscow, and the Secretary of the Moscow House of Peasants had seen to it that he was admitted to the VKhUTEMAS (pronounce: FHUTEMAS). Another student, apprenticed to a Tiflis State publishing-house, had been recommended by it for professional art training at the University. The principle seemed to be: "You have talent, you want to be an artist, we have room in the school. Come in!" Both of these students, and indeed, all who needed it, received a monthly stipend or students' allowance. This was sufficient for all necessities. There was no "means test". The student merely handed in a written application signed by a responsible body such as a Trades Union or co-operative branch or the management of a collective farm. Many students, besides, lived rent free in the hostels attached to the schools and universities. In the VKhUTEMAS hostels, there were several "communes" in which housekeeping was run on a common dead level of contributions. Some students of course had their own private sources of income besides the stipend. Many were supported by their parents and many supported themselves. The publishing-house apprentice, for instance, had a contract with his firm under which he engaged to return and work for them for a stipulated number of years after graduation. On their part they paid him his wages during his years of training.

Vanya, the boy from the country, was rather backward in general education, for his teens had been passed in the hectic and troubled days of the Civil War. Accordingly, like many others similarly placed, he attended the Rabochi Fakultet (*Rab-Fak*) or Workers' Faculty attached to the art school and there he completed his middle school education. This added another year to his training. All institutes and universities had Rab-Faks. They

[1] "Good!"

B

were essential supplements to the educational system in the immediate post-revolutionary period. In 1927 and until 1936, when the new Soviet Constitution came into effect, abolishing many distinctions as no longer necessary, the Soviet state ensured by strict selection that at least 60 per cent. of the students were of working-class parentage. Some 30 per cent. of the remaining available places at the universities and institutes were reserved for youths of peasant origin, the remainder were filled by the sons and daughters of the former so-called upper classes that had been privileged under the old regime: the bourgeoisie, rich farmers who used to employ hired labour, the old bureaucracy, and aristocracy. In this way the Soviet Government ensured that a new generation of technicians and intellectuals would be developed that would, in the stern days that lay ahead, be vitally bound up, by birth and upbringing, with the achievement of the victory of Socialism. Having only just emerged from a regime in which the working classes of town and country had had so few chances of education, the Soviet state considered it necessary for the future to give special educational facilities to men and women of those classes. A guarantee of a majority of vacancies in the institutes and universities was one way of achieving this, and the creation of these Rab-Faks was another and most ingenious way.

In those early years standards of university training were very much lower than they are nowadays. They have in fact been tightened up every year, until to-day they ensure that only really well-qualified specialists pass out as graduates. But there is still an enormous amount of attention paid to enabling talented individuals to get the necessary training even if they have not passed through the ordinary educational channels and, as I shall show later, the system of adult education is very extensive and efficient. But to-day the normal path of the would-be art student leads through the nursery school and elementary school system which are free, then to the technicum, institute, university or Academy. Entrance to these latter is by entrance exam, but elementary school students who have graduated with excellent marks can go straight into the Higher Educational system without taking the entrance exam, even two years after leaving school. Fees lately introduced for the technicums and universities are a more or less emergency, temporary measure, as I feel and shall explain further on, but there is no question of talent being penalised because of these fees even now. In the first place they are very small, and in the second there are numerous scholarships available. All fees are waived in the case of students getting "excellent" marks for two-thirds of their subjects and "good" in the rest. If a boy or girl passes in all subjects, but cannot afford the fees, he or she gets a remission of fees and if necessary a government stipend.

Art training for the Soviet citizen begins early. The so-called "sense-training", in the creches and nurseries for babies under three-and-a-half years old, is a preparation for the enjoyment of artistic experience. The baby learns to make his first steps in the world of sounds and movement and colour by way of learning simple songs and poetry, dancing to music, and colour games. In the kindergarten manual skill and imagination is developed by more advanced games of art, painting, sculpture, learning more complex dances and poetry. Regular schooling begins at eight years of age. And continual consultation between the Trade Unions, the Commissariats of Health and Education ensure regular progression in the child's upbringing.

The "Seven Year School" with education from eight years old to fifteen is the universal elementary school. The "Ten-Year School" general educational curriculum is the same for all children up to fifteen years of age and, with 35,000,000 children at school, would appear to be almost universal to-day. The classes from eight to twelve years with exams beginning at eleven correspond to primary education, from twelve to fifteen they correspond to a middle school education. It is at this stage that the educational facilities begin to differentiate. In the last three classes the young people prepare for the University.

There are special schools for children who show gifts for the arts. Children can enter these schools at the age of eight, but do so more usually at the age of twelve. Art schools for talented children have now been opened by the Leningrad, Moscow, Tiflis and Kiev Academies of Art. In all these schools, the students receive an ordinary general education with extra tuition in art. In their last year of study they give as much as three or more hours a day to their chosen art. All education in these special schools and in primary and middle schools up to the age of fifteen is free. Fees for the three years from fifteen to eighteen amount to about 3 per cent. of the cost. Stipends are granted in case of need.

Nowadays in the schools of the general educational system art training is regarded as an essential part of education, but in the actual school curriculum in the higher classes it occupies only one or two lessons a week. Art training is then organised as an extra-curriculum subject. Not every child can be, and wants to be an artist and it is impossible to provide fully qualified art teachers for every school. Not all specialised training can be crammed into the general curriculum. The children are therefore given the opportunity to make a general acquaintance with art subjects in school time, but are provided with wide facilities for deepening their knowledge and interest in specialised subjects such as art, music, etc. through the multifarious school "circles", and in clubs of the Young Pioneer organisation and the Houses of Children's Culture. Large Pioneer Palaces are available in the larger towns. The Pioneer Palace at Leningrad which is the examplar for all such clubs, has circles for music, literature, painting, the plastic arts, dancing, theatre and engineering crafts, boat building, railway and airplane model construction, zoology, botany and so on. The best qualified instructors the city can provide plan and organise the classes. Leading artists, scientists and technicians are always willing to pay visits. In the ordinary schools the art classes are taken by those teachers who are particularly interested in art and have received special training. Those wishing to train as art teachers can take post-graduate courses available at training centres and art schools and can get instruction and regular assistance from the Moscow Central House for the Artistic Training of Children which specialises in this work, or from the nearest one of the 100 other similar institutions located in other big population centres of the Union. The Moscow Central House and its affiliated centres give instruction to teachers, to art circle leaders, send out syllabuses, typical programmes of work and supply the necessary materials. In addition, schools take advantage of the fact that they can invite practising artists to run courses for the children as part of their social work. The *Moscow News*, for example, was patron of a nearby school. When I became a member of the staff I was invited to take a weekly circle of young artists. The *Moscow News* provided drawing materials and generous supplies of newsprint. When we got into our stride our art circle took on the job of issuing the school wall-newspaper. Such artistic patronage is quite usual between schools and local artists.

Then there are the regular art schools for children, sixty of them with a two-year course. Parents can enrol their children for these courses in addition to their normal education. There is a small fee for tuition.

If the elementary school graduate decides that he wants to take up a career in art, music, theatre art, literature, etc., he can then enrol at one of the 105 vocational and professional technicums which will give him a specialised training and continue his general education from the age of fifteen to twenty. In these technicums all students pay a fee equivalent approximately to £5 a year, which of course is remitted for good marks or for scholarship winners. These schools are attached to the Commissariats for Light or Heavy Industry or Education.

Most students however, in these war years, pass from their middle schools into the free industrial training schools and railway schools. Amateur art circles are a characteristic feature throughout the whole of the secondary educational system. Last year the industrial schools held an Art Olympiad that attracted some several thousand amateur artists and actors.

These facts may be out of date by the time this book is a year or two old. Certainly they will be out of date when the war is over. In the pre-war years of 1932-37, for instance, all education was free and was differently organised. The Soviet educational system is extremely flexible and is designed to answer the needs of the time. Even to-day, in 1943 in the midst of the war, a large number of new musical and theatrical institutions are being opened in forty cities and towns, including Badogushkar Ola, capital of the Mari Autonomous Republic, Syktyvkar, capital of the Komi Republic, Namangan in the Uzbek Republic and also in the Urals and Siberia. And boys and girls over twelve are now taught in separate classes, where before there was universal co-education.

The student who is training to be a professional art worker passes on from one of the technicums of this secondary educational system to the Higher Educational Institutes and Universities of which there are over twenty-nine with over 600,000 students. Entrance to these is by examination. Many of them have Workers Faculties (Rab-Faks) for preliminary or preparatory study. Training lasts for four to five years and in the last two years about 40 per cent. of the student's time is devoted to practical work in his profession. Fees are from 300 to 400 rubles a year which is equivalent to a low average unskilled workers' monthly wage, but here again fees are remitted for good marks and there is a liberal system of stipends and scholarships. In pre-war days all higher education was free. The present principle of fees is clearly a part of state policy designed to attract students without a vocation for art or science away from general higher education and into the industrial trades and professions, the training schools for which remain entirely free.

As before all students are eligible for stipends and there are special bonuses scaled for dependants where workers with families have left the bench and possibly high earnings for the drawing board or easel. But there is no longer a flat stipend rate. Increased sums are awarded for good work, while in the case of flagrant slacking the stipend may be reduced or withdrawn on the recommendation of a stipend committee on which of course sit representatives of the student body. Special provisions are made for married students. The VKhUTEMAS and the Polygraphic Institute which I attended had, like other institutes, special creches for babies. Married women students were given maternity leave and extra time to complete their courses, as well as the usual facilities granted to them by the Trade Unions and state.

The actual art training is by no means the same in all the schools, institutes and academies. I found schools where the art teacher still thought that the best method of teaching drawing was to put something on a table and say "Now children, draw this". But this was exceptional. The Houses for Artistic Training have spread methods which are similar to those used in the best elementary schools here in England. The children are encouraged to give free play to their imaginations; to approach art without self consciousness, to paint, act, recite as if this were a normal part of their life, as indeed it should be. The schoolboy poet is admired just as much as the school football team captain or prize-model maker. I once got one of the best definitions of the art of drawing from a Soviet five-year-old: "I take a think and then I draw a line around it!"

Fairies and monsters have their place in these children's drawings, but the modern Soviet child's art is, I think, characterised by its intense awareness of contemporary life and the romance of modern science, technics, the drama of the war. It is only at a much later stage that the young art student is encouraged and taught to refine down his perceptions, consciously approach problems of compositions, perspective, anatomy and so on. This is the work of the more advanced classes, the Technicums, Institutes and Academies. The methods of approach to these higher studies is also not the same in all institutes. It depends on the individual teachers, the traditions of the schools.

The Leningrad Art Academy, housed in the vast building of the Tsar's Academy on the banks of the Neva, holds closest to the technical tenets of academicism. In the 1920's the Moscow Academy was the stronghold of the various modern tendencies such as Cézannism, Cubism, Constructivism. There was the most lively controversy between Moscow and Leningrad on the modern approach to realism. The other academies such as the national academies of the Ukraine, Uzbekistan, Turkestan or Georgia, naturally stress the development of their own traditional national cultures within the context of socialism.

It is the common and characteristic features of Soviet art schools that are of greater interest to-day. In the first place the most valuable advance has been made in developing the are students' general educational equipment. This has been brought

up to the highest university standards in social-economic theory,
in philosophy, art history and aesthetic theory.

Every student gets a good grounding in mathematics, biology,
geography, social economic world history, in political economy
and the economic policy of the Soviet Union. Every Soviet
University graduate is given a good grounding in philosophy: in
dialectrical-materialism, the history of philosophy and Marxism-
Leninism. In the sphere of art, besides the usual technical dis-
ciplines, the student studies art history and the sociology of art,
that is, the study of the various styles of art that are associated
with stages of social development.

The student participates actively in the lectures, discussions
and stimulating controversies that accompany the analysis of the
latest trends of Western art in the university debating society,
the Communist Academy, or at the big meetings organised by
the various artists' organisations. He studies the theoretical and
practical tenets of impressionism, surrealism, and the new monu-
mentalism of industrial America. He takes part in the debates on
the role and style of art in the socialist Soviet Union, and on the
question of which elements of the past are adaptable and which
have no valuable application to-day. He is constantly recommended to "master the art of the past".

These studies and the various social activities into which the
student is drawn, teach him to conceive life as a whole, as a
"unity". He learns to see art as part of life. The idea of "Art
for Art's sake" is regarded as nonsense in the Soviet state. The
Soviet youth is definitely "materialistic" in the sense that he sees
life as something to be lived, and lived to the full, and knows that
art is one of the ways in which man achieves this fuller life.

Soviet university training is designed to inspire the youth with
a keen sense of social responsibility.

People who doubt the feasibility of socialism, and still more of
communism, usually trot out the question "If there is no
profit motive or motive of direct personal gain, what will make
people work?" The Soviet Union—and its educational system in
school, university, art and propaganda—supplies the answer. It
shows that, in a socialist state, in an amazingly short space of time,

"THE GERMANS' GUIDE IN THE CAUCASUS"
(Pen, brush and Indian ink)   *by the Kukryniksi*

THE OATH OF THE GUERRILLAS

(Oil painting)

INTERROGATION OF TWO COMMUNISTS (CIVIL WAR SCENE)

by Boris Johanson

THE CHAIRWOMAN

(Oil painting)   *by Georgi Ryazhsky*

the community develops a greatly heightened sense of social responsibility that rapidly supersedes the "profit motive" and proves itself superior to it as an incentive to work and creative activity. This is no longer a theoretical "possibility". The Soviet "experiment" has proved it in practice ... in a stand-up battle with the uttermost development of the "profit motive"—fascism. The great Stakhanovite movement was the most amazing manifestation of this new development of civic sense. The "profit motive" is indeed so discredited in the U.S.S.R. that a student could be expelled from a university or institute if it were proved that he was animated solely by the desire to "make money" or "make a name for himself". At the very least, a "careerist"— that is a man who seeks his own advancement at the public expense—runs the risk of social ostracism. The whole influence of school and teachers and associated organisations is designed to instil into the student the consciousness that he is studying, not for his own primary benefit, but for that of the whole human community.

I had not been at the VKhUTEMAS three weeks before I myself felt the force of this influence, and I must admit that I needed it. Having hitherto received an education whose keynote was "learn-to-make-a-living and the devil take the hindmost", and also having been brought up in fairly easy circumstances, I naturally gravitated towards the lighter-headed members of the student body, that small percentage of "golden youth", the sons and daughters of some of the old-style intelligentsia and NEPmen. These were still motivated by the idea of "having a good time", and this really meant wasting an inordinate amount of good time in the city's cafés and particularly in the "*Dom Gertsena*", an artists' club that was the last refuge of Moscow's remaining "Bohemians". My escapades with the "gang" quickly became notorious. I gained a considerable amount of "fame" by carrying off the Charleston Championship of Moscow in the contests of 1927. This was hardly the way to behave if one came to the centre of world advancement for the purpose of studying how to better mankind! The denouement came when one day during the break I was doing the Charleston on the stage of the great hall with our local college blonde and glamour girl, Vera. A loud proletarian voice suddenly ripped through the strains of jazz:

"Hi, Comrade! And what about the Chinese Revolution?" it said.

My feet hesitated and I trod heavily on Vera's toes.

Bohemianism among artists is of course a dead letter in present-day U.S.S.R. It was a sort of protective camouflage assumed by artists in the intolerable conditions in which they lived in Paris and other cities over the turn of the century. With their secure position in Russia artists have no need of such camouflage.

The spirit of socialism, brotherhood and service permeates the teachings and indeed the whole organisation of school and university. In addition to purely scholastic activities, there are numerous other organisations which help to develop the students' civic sense and organisational talents. Every student belongs to one or several of these societies. I myself at one time belonged to no less than eight! The names of these many organisations are self-explanatory: The Red Aid Society to help Victims of Fascism Abroad, the Proletarian Tourist Society (a youth hostel movement with several million members and hundreds of hostels), the Artists' Union, the Union of Printing Trades Workers, the Union of Workers of Art (all students are eligible for full Trade Union membership), the Communist Party, the Young Communist League (which is not a Party, but, as the junior training group of the Communist Party, attracts all the most vital and serious elements among the youth). Then of course there are many special study and sport groups. The eight million strong OSOAVIAKHIM, (Society for Air and Chemical Defence), runs courses in the operation of mechanical vehicles, parachute jumping and gliding, sniping, flying and map-reading and A.R.P., and offers facilities for the gaining of the *Ready for Labour and Defence* badge which shows that the wearer has passed tests in running, ski-ing, swimming, jumping, etc. In addition to assisting toward development of various aspects of Soviet policy, these organisations train up thousands of part-time administrators and organisers who learn their job in school and university as chairmen, treasurers and secretaries of branch groups (part of their "social work"). The Soviet student passes naturally from a position of responsibility in his school society to the larger responsibility of local Soviet Councils, Communist Party Committees or professional Trades Unions.

One very important result of their training as socially minded citizens is that Soviet students find it much less of a hardship to return to their native towns in the provinces or Republics when their training is over in the capitals. Talent is thus spread advantageously throughout the land instead of being overconcentrated at the capitals. In passing it may be of interest to mention that our glamour blonde, Vera, afterwards found her niche in Soviet life by becoming fashion designer to the Moscow "Atelier Modes". She had been undoubtedly the best-dressed girl at school.

The system of "Production Practice" is an essential element in this training for social service and for citizenship. Students do not learn to make pictures only in their studios. While still learning, indeed as part of their learning, they are actually commissioned to paint club-room decorations or murals for city squares during public festivals. While still at school they are sent to work in commercial studios, workshops or in printing houses on the same level as fully-fledged Trade Union craftsmen.

While still a second-year student I worked for two months in the Soviet Mint, where banknotes and stamps are printed and the finest reproduction work is done. I had ample opportunity to try my hand at every process of book and newspaper artists' work during practice with one of the leading publishing firms. I learned the job of high-pressure daily newspaper work at first hand. I worked at the "Ogonyok" Publishing House which produces over two dozen weekly and monthly magazines and newspapers. I worked in the departments for processing blocks for printing in all techniques. I worked in the editorial offices. I saw newspaper production from all sides. I made friends with many of the artists and writers employed by these papers. They, and the editors and technical men, gave me innumerable professional tips that no art school could teach. I got several commissions for drawings, and even before I graduated, I had arranged to work for one of their new publications—the *Moscow News*—for which I later became cartoonist and art editor. Many other students made similar contracts during their months of practice. Those who had not found jobs for themselves by graduation day were given lists of places to choose from. One group of students who had built up a working co-operative asked for and received a loan advance from the Commissariat of Education to set up a co-operative art studio of their own.

In my last year, I spent my "practice" at *Pravda*, the most important newspaper in the Soviet Union, the official organ of the Communist Party. *Pravda's* circulation and that of its satellite newspapers and magazines run into millions. It is the most influential newspaper in the world, but its doors were opened wide to me by my student's "practice pass", and I was paid Trade Union wages to boot. This was the American "earn while you learn" idea on an entirely different basis. I worked through the offices. One of my assignments was to study its organisational structure. I found time to try my hand at newspaper photography and my practice pass brought me to the front row at great demonstrations and performances, "shooting" well-known personages, like Kalinin or Felix Kohn, at close quarters and from all angles. I was sent out on an assignment to photograph Krupskaya, Lenin's widow. I found her in the offices of the Central Executive Committee of the Party, chairing a women's delegate meeting. She posed for me with the delegates in the break. I hit the *Pravda* front page with a three column picture. It was a foggy drizzly day when the workers' parades went to greet the opening of the sixteenth Party Congress at the Bolshoi Theatre in Moscow. One by one *Pravda's* ace photographers came back to the department reporting "Fog!" I had already gone back to my room at the "Metropole" that overlooked the Bolshoi, when a lucky break of sunshine gave us just the picture we needed. The famous cartoonist Deni later used my photo for a montage cartoon-poster.

Here in the *Pravda* offices I made friends with Boris Yefimov. Deni, Moor, Ganf, Rotov and Yeliseyev, men who had already made cartoon history. One morning I ran across Fred Ellis, the veteran American cartoonist, who had come over to draw for

Pravda. It was Fred Ellis who gave me my best lessons in art, and later, when I edited the art pages of the *Moscow News*, I got all these artists to draw for us. This was no easy feat, because they are always working at full pressure. Yefimov, for instance, turns out two front-page cartoons a day for the *Izvestia* and *Red Star*, besides book and magazine work.

During this same practice period at the *Pravda*, a colleague of mine got a contract to join the photo-department. The job was held open for her until she graduated.

These practice periods don't mean just looking on to see how things are done. As soon as you are considered competent to take an individual assignment you are given the same blame for failure or praise for success as any regular member of the staff. These are real jobs. There is thus no hard and fast boundary between "school" and "life". It is all one. Young men and women get an early sense of oneness with the great world of work and achievement. They see themselves as part of the great plan of "socialist construction". This linking up of study and practice, this early mixing with the basic workers of the industry and participation in Trade Union life, obviates all those infantile disorders that usually attend the ordeal of "going out into life" among university students of the West.

Another valuable result of these practice periods is that, in going through various jobs in their professions and following out complete industrial and art processes, the students get an integrated understanding of their professions and a clearer idea of what they really want to specialise in and what they need to learn. For instance, while I was inclined to be impatient when I had to do the technical work of printing, I noticed that other students, who had seemed better and keener artists than I, got more and more interested in technical processes and research and gradually dropped their drawing to specialise in technology.

In those days the VKhUTEMAS had faculties for Polygraphic, Mural and Ceramic Art, Sculpture, Easel Painting, Textile, Architecture and Theatre Design. Each section had its own particular type of production practice. Just as the students of the Oil Institute go to work in the oil wells of Baku, or future

mining engineers cut coal in the Donbas, so the textile and ceramic students work at various mills and potteries, and the theatre
designers work at various state theatres.

In 1930 this process of linking up study and training with
actual production was carried a step further. The Polygraphic
Faculty of the VKhUTEMAS was transformed into an independent Polygraphic Institute catering for the whole Soviet
printing industry. It now has branches in most of the important
Republics, and is directed and advised by the heads and experts
of the industry, who are able to plan the rate of expansion of the
institute and the type of training suitable to the requirements of
the industry. Similar arrangements have now been made for the
Textile and Ceramic Institutes.

The advantages of this are obvious. When my younger sister
became a student of the Cinema Institute in 1932, she actually
had her lectures and tuition on the premises of one of the biggest
Moscow film studios. From the very first day she found herself
part and parcel of film making, and literally "grew up" in that
industry and art. Another of my sisters, who was studying dancing
and theatrical production at the Theatre Institute, went through
her "production practice" behind the scenes of chosen theatres,
watching the creation of productions from the script-reading up
to the finished performance. In the course of one practice, she
worked behind the scenes of the great Moscow Bolshoi Theatre
of Opera and Ballet, and borrowed this vast auditorium one night
after the regular performance to give a dance concert of her own.
I mention this as an indication of the interest that is lavished on
the "practising students". There is not the faintest suspicion of
them being treated as "necessary evils" in industry. On the
contrary, they become the special care of personnel managers,
and their progress is watched by the whole of the regular collective
of workers in factory, studio or theatre, as if they were the enterprise's own apprentices—which of course they are.

As a further significant sidelight on Soviet methods of art
education I should relate that several years after I graduated, I
decided that I needed a further course of drawing from the model
and in water-colour and oil painting. After a five-minute inter-

view with the new director of the Institute—who happened to be my old faculty head—I was re-enrolled as a student for a post-graduate course. Naturally I paid no additional fees. This is quite a normal feature of the educational system. The student is looked upon as a "product" of the technicum or institute, as so much "human capital", the most valuable "capital" in the Soviet Union. If there are any defects in his training that detract from his worth as a specialist, then it is the duty of the educational system to remedy those defects.

SAVIOURS OF CULTURE

Cartoon by A. Kanevsky.

"See how many valuables we've saved from the fire in the museum."
"But is the museum burning?"
"Not yet. But we'll soon see to that!"

III

ARTISTS AT WORK

Formerly (the intelligentsia) had to serve the wealthy classes, for it had no alternative. To-day it must serve the people, for there are no longer any exploiting classes. And that is precisely why it is now an equal member of Soviet society in which, side by side with the workers and peasants, pulling together with them, it is engaged in building the new, classless, socialist society.

STALIN.

★

BY GRADUATION day, most of the students were already assigned to jobs. Many had obtained contracts during their "practice periods", just as I had signed on with the "Ogonyok" publishing house. The lay-out men, photographers, various grades of printing trades technicians, ceramic and textile designers, architects and industrial designers had considerable choice as to their place of work. In a period when every branch of Soviet industry and art was expanding rapidly every year there was indeed a shortage of skilled men. Unemployment in the Soviet Union was abolished in 1928.

With my previous experience of newspaper work and cartooning I had little difficulty in settling in on the *Moscow News*. I planned and laid out the art pages at a monthly salary. I also drew cartoons for an extra fee, and what with illustrations for books and other magazines and papers, I was soon busy and prosperous enough to devote a fair amount of time to painting and further study.

As a member of the Printing Trades Union (Artists Section), my rates of pay were fixed according to a recognised scale settled by mutual agreement between the Trades Union and the Industry. I could certainly never grumble that I was ever paid too little. Fees, indeed, for drawings and cartoons were generous. There was never any attempt to beat down prices because I was a beginner and, of course none of that sordid bargaining that is so disagreeable a feature of journalistic life outside the Union. Deni or Yefimov, the stars of the cartoon world, received four or five times the rate I got for a drawing, but I rather think their high rate was to protect them from being overworked! Yefimov was always up to the ears in work. He is one of the fastest cartoonists I know of. Long and intimate contact with the most astute political minds in the country—there was nobody that was anybody that he didn't know—and a razor-keen brain and eye gave him an astonishing knack of picking on the key feature of the day as he skimmed through the morning papers. The *Izvestia* editors on occasion would send him round a chit if there was special news on hand. In a few hours or sometimes minutes he would have his drawings ready. Like the famous French artist Caran d'Ache, he would lay out the composition roughly, on ordinary paper, place a piece of transparent drawing paper over it and then draw in the figures rapidly and easily. He said that he never knew what it was "not to have an idea". Collections of his cartoons make an astonishingly accurate history of the times.

Ganf and Rotov were so busy that they had a special "theme man" working with them at *Pravda*. They used to draw all the morning at home and in the afternoon about 5 p.m. come to the *Pravda*. Their "theme man", had already gone into consultation with the editors and over tea he would present them with a list of themes and sometimes "ideas". An hour or so after this the cartoon itself would be ready for the presses. Most of the other artists worked at the same high pressure. The Young Communist paper—*Komsomolskaya Pravda*—had three young cartoonists on its pay role.

Here is a sidelight on the Soviet attitude to this question of pay. The *Moscow News* in its early days was run for the "Ogonyok" by a group of American and English journalists and myself, a Chinese. Most of us were not Party members, but all were much inspired by the idealistic doctrines of socialism, so that we soon joined in the socialist emulation movement to "raise quality and lower costs". One way we discovered of lowering costs was by

c

taking small salaries ourselves and paying our contributors on a like scale. This went unnoticed for exactly a month—newspaper accounts are made up on a monthly basis. Then one day I met Yefimov who had done some drawings for us. "You're not paying me my correct rate", he said. The firm's cashier also noticed it and so evidently did other contributors, for the next day the local Party secretary explained to us gently that this method of cutting costs was not only "not done" but was illegal even though we ourselves had agreed to take less wages. On the other hand, once we had got our wages, of course there was nothing to prevent us from voluntarily "ploughing them back into the State", as it were, in the form of State loans, gifts and so on.

All workers in the "Ogonyok" publishing house were members of the same Trade Union section, which had its own elected whole-time secretary and voluntary executive committee. It was this committee that took up all questions of wages, hours and conditions of work with the management of the enterprise; it also saw to our vacations (I had three weeks a year with pay), it organised our rest home in a delightful villa in the pine forests outside Moscow; arranged for our holidays or rest cures in the Crimea and Caucasian resorts, and provided us with free medical attention.

Later I left the staff of the *Moscow News* and became a freelance artist and critic working for several publishing houses, but I retained my membership of the "Ogonyok" Trade Union section because most of my work still went to its publications, and I retained all my privileges of membership. I paid my dues to the section and when sick or on holiday I received two-thirds of my average monthly earnings. This would be full wages after five years employment. At sixty I would be eligible for full old-age pension.

Like everyone else in the Soviet Union I did voluntary "social work", which was unpaid, as well as my ordinary paid work. There is no compulsion to do this "social work" except the compulsion of public opinion and one's own social consciousness. If I didn't do it I would be classed as a "skurnik"—a fellow who cared only for his own interests, that is, a very disreputable individual. I usually did the work which interested me most. When there was a "Subbotnik"—voluntary rest-day work—to help on the building of the Metro underground railway, instead of digging, I helped to put out a wall newspaper and drew pictures of leading shockbrigaders, but one severe winter, when the cold threatened to freeze the potatoes we had contracted for at the collective farm which supplied our canteen, the whole staff turned out to a man to save the crop.

On another occasion I was asked by the Moscow Committee of the Young Communist League to put out a wall-newspaper at one of their Congresses. At one time or other pretty well every leading cartoonist in Moscow came down to lend a hand during the two days of meetings. They would drop in for an hour or two, listen to the speeches or read the stenographic reports, turn out their drawings at lightning speed, and these would be mounted by the lay-out men on the gradually lengthening wall newspaper in the vestibule, a witty and artistic comment on the proceedings. This was typical cartoonists' "social work".

As part of my social work I also ran an art class for the children of the school that our office took under its "patronage"; and at the great people's festivals I painted banners and invented mechical poster toys which were carried in the demonstrations. On another occasion I did three weeks art work drawing Heroes of Labour, making wall newspapers, posters and signs to aid the Metro workers.

In the early nineteen-thirties, before drastic economies were instituted for war-time needs, the "Ogonyok" spent hundreds of rubles on its festival decorations. The big Moscow factories and trusts spent thousands of rubles on theirs, but then their marching columns were usually thousands strong and they often carried very elaborate decorations—with models of the planes and machines they built, examples of their textiles, finely designed banners, portraits of their popular leaders. In the summer parades the columns of marching youngsters carried bouquets and garlands of flowers, so that each square looked like a Covent Garden flower show. The great mass of this decorative work was done by amateur artists or professionals in their spare time, but

leading professionals were commissioned to design the more
important decorations. The Red Square, the Theatre Square,
the Square of the Revolution, Gorky Street were always centres
of attraction, and crowds in their thousands would visit them
after the demonstrations of the day. Huge murals decorated the
sides of the surrounding buildings; constructions filled the space
in each square. After 1933 it became the custom to clear all the
shop windows on the long Gorky Street and fill them with the
best examples of contemporary art or models of new and recon-
structed homes and cities, thus turning the whole street into a
vast public art gallery. Moscow *en fête* on May Day, 1934, was
an unforgettably joyous spectacle. Besides the festival decorations of the streets, there were bumper numbers of newspapers
and magazines, new plays, symphonies, poems and songs. Each
great festival is an artistic event of the first importance, and the
demand for art work, for the five great annual festivals alone, provides a permanent and stable inspiration for the artist of every
speciality. Most of the art work done for the big state trusts and
factories, the city, town and village Soviets, the Red Army and
various Commissariats is handsomely paid for.

In those days I lived the normal life of a young artist in the
Union. I had my own flat, lived and dressed comfortably,
saw most of the new productions in theatre and cinema,
bought all the new books I wanted (books of course are cheap
in the U.S.S.R.), dined and danced at clubs, or occasionally
hotels, toured in the Crimea, the Caucausus, the Ukraine, or
Leningrad in my holidays, spent pleasant week-ends at our
firm's country villa near Moscow, played tennis or swam in
the summer and ski-ed or skated in the winter. I served on
various committees and did social work in my spare time.
Twice or three times a week in winter time I attended various
courses; philosophy, economics, politics. I earned about
1,000 rubles a month. I received from 75 to 100 rubles for a
cartoon or illustration; 300 rubles for a book jacket; 400-500
rubles for a poster.

In 1933 advertising came to be more widely employed. The
Commissariat for Food, for example, began to popularise many

new foods, such as rhubarb and corn-flakes, and the new factories of the Five-Year Plans were anxious to build up the prestige of their Soviet Trade Marks. There was a phenomenal increase in the number of newspapers, magazines and books which demanded a constant supply of jackets and illustrations. But I have said enough to show that the newspaper, decorative or commercial artist is in great demand in the modern Soviet Union, and well rewarded. (I am here speaking of normal peacetime conditions, of course. I will deal with the war later.)

What becomes of the easel artist, the painter of landscapes or portraits in oils, the still-life painter—the men who in London, Paris or New York have the normal peacetime reputation of being chronically hard up—unless they have become one of the relatively few who have "succeeded"? In the U.S.S.R. the easel painter as a narrow specialist appears to be disappearing. This is not part of any set policy—life is making it so. The life and interests of the artist have been broadened. He is called upon to undertake such varied and inspiring work that he is becoming as versatile as the artist guildsman in the heyday of the Italian Renaissance.

Williams, for instance, is a fine painter—but he also designs some of the finest sets for Moscow and Leningrad theatres. His *Pickwick Papers* decors are unsurpassed. He has also illustrated many books, designed posters and murals.

Deineka is one of the finest of the younger painters. He is no less noted as a poster artist and mural painter and has now exhibited his first sculptures. The three artists known as the "Kukryniksi" (Kuprianov, Krylov, and Nikolai Sokolov) are lithographers, poster artists, painters, fresco designers, miniature sculptors, superb puppeteers and designers of half a dozen theatre productions, including Mayakovsky's *Bed Bug* at the Meyerhold. These three artists received their entire art education —as did Williams and Deineka—in Soviet art schools—they were one course ahead of me at the VKhUTEMAS—and made their name as caricaturists while they were still in the school studios. Their series of caricatures of leading Soviet personalities, which I saw them working on as their diploma work, is already a landmark in Soviet caricature. I was lucky enough to see the beginnings of this original artistic personality. Kuprianov and Krylov came together from the same technicum at Taskhent and joined the VKhUTEMAS in 1921. Here they met Sokolov. Sokolov and Kuprianov studied under Mturich, a fine old draughtsman, and Kupreanov, a lithographer, water-colour artist and enthusiastic admirer of Daumier and Toulouse-Lautrec. Krylov studied painting under Osmerkin. It was joint work on the wall newspapers of the school that first drew them together, and their unique friendship, built up about the home of Kuprianov and his charming artist wife, is the basis of their "collective". To-day 'Kukryniksi' is a definite artistic personality compounded of their three talents. A drawing signed with that pseudonym may be actually the work of one pair of hands, but it is always the product of three brains. Sometimes they all work on a single drawing or painting. When they did a caricature of me one night the drawing board passed from hand to hand. The "likeness" was perfect though they drew me from three separate corners of the room. It was impossible to say where one's line ended and another's began. The triple entity 'Kukryniksi' to-day is 100 years old with a brilliant future still ahead of him.

To take some of the older generation: Favorsky, one of the world's leading wood engravers, was a teacher of distinction (Deineka, the painter, and Goncharov, Pimenov, and many other engravers, were his pupils), a stage designer, painter, fresco artist and architect. My own teacher at the VKhUTEMAS, the late Pavel Nevinsky, was the leader of a whole school of Soviet etching, an expert water-colourist and the designer of the famous "Princess Turandot" sets for the Vakhtangov production, that marked a revolution in theatre design. Sergei Gerasimov is not only one of the best painters, he is also a first-class illustrator and teacher. Moor, the veteran cartoonist, designed some of the finest and gayest street decorations Moscow has seen.

There are, of course, many artists who still specialise in painting as an almost exclusive profession. These are such artists as Lekht, the landscape painter—he is very fully occupied nowadays making industrial landscapes. Johanson is essentially a painter.

He thinks in colour. Ryazhsky too. He has specialised in painting the new typical types of Soviet life. Radimov has long been known as a painter of the familiar old Russian landscape. To-day he is working on an extended plan, with the aid of the Soviet government and the Artists' Co-operative, to make a picture record of historic places in Russia.

Nikolai Korin, whose ancestors for scores of years were ikon painters of old Russia, is himself to-day, besides being a secular painter of note—his paintings of Gorky, who "discovered" him are well-known—an ecclesiastical painter as well. He has just finished a large portrait figure of the late Patriarch Sergius and is now working on one of the biggest religious paintings ever made in Moscow, a huge historic group portrait of outstanding Russian religious leaders and saints.

But these are the successful artists who are able to choose their work from an abundance of interesting commissions. What of the painter of average talent—of the man whose talent takes time to develop? How does the average Soviet painter pass from the schools to a successful and useful career as a professional painter?

*   *   *

THE ARTISTS' CO-OPERATIVE

During his years of training, the artist painter, like any skilled technician, also does his periods of production practice. For his practice he goes to the big clubs, commercial studios or Parks of Culture and designs banners, large-scale murals, paintings and decorations. Very many artists make this type of work their career. It is an interesting, busy and lucrative profession and if an artist on leaving art school is not able to set up immediately as a full-time specialist easel painter of "small forms" the knowledge that he gains of these large-scale popular forms of art is quite sufficient to keep him going financially while continuing his easel painting in his studio, although this sort of work may not be quite the sort of specialised work that he wants eventually to do. I myself think that the large-scale decorative work that clubs, theatres and festivals demand is an excellent training for every artist. And in a characteristically Soviet way, the fact that this work is so intimately connected with the peoples' everyday life, adds to the social esteem in which the artist doing it is held.

Students are also commissioned, on a professional basis as part of their practice, to paint portraits of heroes and Stakhanovites, factory or collective farm landscapes, etc. A large number of travelling commissions (kommandirovki) are also available for students as well as post-graduate scholarships, so that—coupled with the large demand for pictures—it is an exceptional case where an artist, who wants to be an easel painter and is trained for that art, has to do something else for a living until "he wins recognition". A Soviet artist "wins recognition" when he enters the art school.

As a member of RABIS—the Workers of Art Trade Union— which he can join as a student, the artist's wages are protected; he is assured of proper medical attention and an allowance if ill or convalescent. If he is unemployed he is entitled to an unemployment allowance. But this is a remote contingency, I never met an unemployed Soviet artist. The demand for art work is far greater than the supply. The T.U. also provides loans at low interest rates if they are needed.

On graduation from art school or Academy nearly every artist applies for membership of the *Khudozhnik*, the Artists' Co-operative and is accepted on payment of an initial subscription of ten rubles, and the recommendations of two members. His annual dues are in proportion to his income. The Co-operative then becomes his agent and performs many other useful services for him. In the first place, it supplies him with painting materials of all descriptions made in its own laboratories and factories. If he is given a special commission he can get suitable materials imported from abroad. It rents him an excellent studio-flat as and when this becomes available in the specially-built artists' centre near Moscow's Sokolniki Park. It also buys outright, exhibits or sells his work on commission in its chain of exhibition galleries and art goods stores in all the main cities of the Union. The Co-operative in Moscow arranges several large exhibitions every year as well as regular Spring and Autumn Salons. A

TALES OF ANIMALS BY LEO TOLSTOY
(Woodcut)   *by Favorsky*

ILLUSTRATION TO "GRANDPA NAZAI AND THE RABBITS"
(Wash drawing)   *by Sergei Boyim*

PEASANT REVOLT, FROM "THE LIFE OF LENIN"

(Woodcut)   *Peter Staronoso*

"NOW WHAT ARE YOU WORRYING ABOUT?"
ILLUSTRATION TO "HISTORY OF A CITY", BY SALTIKOV-SHCHEDRIN
(Lithograph) *by Alexander Samokhvalov*

44

TWO LITHOGRAPH DRAWINGS FROM S. MIKHALKOV'S "SO", A CHILDREN'S POEM

Commission of 8 per cent. is taken on all sales. The Co-operative also arranges discussions, lectures and post-graduate courses on art and the social sciences.

Artists can also arrange to contract their work to the Co-operative. An artist wishing to do so presents a plan of work for the year, and a selection of his drawings and pictures, to a committee which decides on the probable annual commercial value of his work, and on the basis of this estimate pays him a fixed monthly allowance. This committee of experts is elected annually by the Co-operative members. At the end of the year, or at stated intervals, the artist sends his work in. It is sold through the Co-operative galleries and, if the total price received is in excess of the amount advanced to the artist, this addition is placed to his credit. If there is a debit balance, it is carried over to the next year's account. A permanent debit naturally leads to a reduction of the artist's monthly allowance. In the R.S.F.S.R. alone, over 400 artists are working under contracts that relieve them of all material need.

The Co-operative also arranges commissions for its artist members. If the Government of a Republic such as Turkmenistan or Azerbaidzhan, of a city Soviet such as Moscow or Tiflis, wants to award a commission for the decoration of a library or school or station, the artists' Co-operative will advise them in the choice of an artist. If an expedition is going to the Pamirs or the Arctic and wants an artist, the Co-operative will recommend the best man for the job. On such *kommandirovki* the artist receives about 600 rubles a month, in addition to travelling expenses, and the client commissions a set number of drawings or pictures. Whatever else he may do remains the property of the artist—subject of course to security or other special considerations which will be stated in the contract. In an average year about 500 artists receive such *kommandirovki*. The Co-operative receives a small commission for its services, usually 8 per cent. Its total capital to-day is something over Rs. 100,000,000. It began with an initial loan of Rs. 15,000, and later received another loan of Rs. 8,000,000 from the Central Communal Bank. The extent of the Co-operative's artistic activities is evidenced by its turnover: over

45,000,000 rubles in 1940. Just over 10 per cent. of this sum, or exactly 4,600,000 rubles, directly concerned the sale of pictures. The rest was made up by the sale of various art materials, artistic household knick-knacks such as cigarette-ash trays, writing sets, fine fabrics, lamp shades, embroideries, etc., made in the Co-operative's own studios and workshops, reproductions of well-known statues, busts of popular leaders, and so on. This financial result seems profitable enough, but it earned the censure of the artists' governing council, which decided that the sale of pictures and reproductions should play a bigger role, both absolute and relative, in the future activities of the co-operative.

In dealing with sales of pictures, it is interesting to note that, in the immediate pre-war period, sales to private individuals amounted to only a small percentage of total sales, though the number of privately bought water-colours, drawings, etchings, wood-cuts, paintings and sculpture was steadily increasing. The big orders come from the various governments, commissariats, local soviets and trusts, Trade Union and other collective bodies.

When the Red Army approached its fifteenth birthday in 1932, it decided to commemorate the date by a great art exhibition. The only demand on would-be exhibitors was that their work should deal with some aspect of Red Army life or history, or the defence of the U.S.S.R. Hundreds of artists participated. Some sent in finished work, others presented sketches of canvases they proposed to do. A friend of mine, the young artist Dorokhov, who had visited the Far Eastern Territory, sent in the sketches he had made there together with a plan of a canvas illustrating an episode of the Vladivostok guerilla movement against the White Guards and Intervention armies. His idea was accepted and he was commissioned, with expenses paid, to travel East and complete the picture. The Red Army Defence Council bought hundreds of paintings, sculptures and drawings valued at one million rubles. These were exhibited in Moscow and other centres and then placed in Red Army museums, headquarters, barracks and clubs. A million people visited the exhibition in the first three months.

A special illustrated album was issued for the jubilee. Stalin, one of the editors, looking over the proofs, was so struck by the Kukryniksi's work that he ordered double the number of pictures originally commissioned from them.

Two years later an even bigger exhibition was organised by the Commissariat for Heavy Industry under the general theme title "The Industry of Socialism". Here again millions of rubles were spent on preparation. Another of my young artist friends who had once visited Igarka, the Arctic port, while on a "proletarian" tour, sent in sketches and a lay-out for a large canvas. His proposal was accepted by the organisers. The work was commissioned, a substantial advance was made and he received special facilities to return to Igarka and complete the canvas.

The latest such exhibition to be announced was for 1941, when the theme was to have been "Our Native Land". This naturally had to be postponed on account of the war, and an exhibition on the theme of "The Patriotic War" was held in place of it in the autumn of 1943. Such exhibitions are usually announced a year or two ahead in order to allow for careful preparation. Many artists' commissions come in addition from factories and institutes which often order portraits or landscapes of their sites and buildings, records of their work. There is, for example, a truly amazing picture record of the great Dnieper Dam construction. This is like the work done under the " Recording Britain" scheme.

The Soviet Artists' Co-operative, as the artist reader will particularly appreciate, completely supersedes the "artist's agent" of other countries and performs all his functions far more completely and far more economically. It does away with all the obnoxious traits of the racket known as "dealing in pictures". The Co-operative frees the artist of most of the business worry of art as a profession and he is able to devote all his energy to creative work.

Prices of pictures of course depend on the picture itself, its size, terms of special contracts and the prestige of the artist. Values vary greatly and so do prices. The average price paid for a picture sold by the artists' Co-operative some years ago was 500 rubles. It is probably higher to-day. Paintings usually range from about 300 to 10,000 rubles. Water-colours fetch from 150 to 300 rubles. Sculptural work may range to over 30,000 rubles for a figure or group. A Co-operative contract will give the artist an assured income of between 500 to 2,000 rubles a month, which is sufficient for normal everyday needs.

All these "contracts", *kommandirovki* and ordinary commissions are all very well for the successful and popular artist, or for the "average" talented artist with average skill, but, I am often asked, "what about the artist who is slow in developing?"

As regards the artist who is slow in developing, I am sure that there is no other land which could give him a fairer chance of development. For instance, I met the young artist D. while I was at the VKhUTEMAS. He was still finishing up under a certain "Left" artist who assured his students that, since verisimilitude to nature was now the undisputed province of the photographer, there was no need for the painter to study anatomy and all that. He could concentrate on "pure form". The result of this tuition was that D. and several other students were acutely conscious, as they approached their graduation in 1929, that their technical training was sadly lopsided. The tide of art had swung from the formal abstractions of "Constructivism" to Realism. They were healthy young Soviet citizens and they wanted to paint the pulsating new life of socialism that was growing up before them, but, lacking a knowledge of the technique of realism, they were frustrated. In this crisis a meeting of the faculty and students was held. It was decided that these students be given every opportunity to continue their studies while they trained themselves afresh for their task as Soviet artists. They and their talent and training— such as it was—was regarded as so much socialist "capital", part of the national wealth, and as such had to be husbanded and tended. All of these young artists were awarded contracts that gave them ample time for intensive study. They were given studios in the House of the Artists, and to-day at least three of them are in the leading rank of young painters.

Exhibition juries and the artist-elected committees for Co-operative contracts naturally have the right to reject pictures or sculptures for political, moral or artistic reasons. Artists, of course, can sell their own pictures or other work privately if they are so inclined.

Somehow there has grown up the idea that, of necessity, art in a Socialist country must be lacking in variety of styles. But a glance through Soviet art publications will show the rich variety of individual or group style developed in recent years. Compare, for instance, the styles of such painters as Brodsky, Gerasimov, Sternberg, the Kukryniksi, Deineka or Tishler, Lebedev and Pimenov. I got to know most of these artists: some of them were my intimate friends. As art critic for *Moscow News*, I saw much of their work. The late Isaac Brodsky was a painstaking naturalist, whose work would be acceptable to any Academy. He was held in particular esteem because he was one of the few leading Russian Academicians to give whole-hearted support to the new Soviet regime from the first days of October. He later became head of the Soviet Art Academy; in 1932 this was established in the same palace on the banks of the Neva that had housed the original Imperial Academy. He made many valuable documentary portraits of the revolutionary leaders, and his work was immensely popular among the Soviet farmers. Gerasimov belongs to the strong Russian realist tradition of landscape painters, stemming from Levitan; Sternberg brings to Soviet themes a vision highly coloured by the cosmopolitan art of Paris post-impressionism. Lebedev of Leningrad is an essentially urban painter, elegant, sophisticated, an inveterate experimenter in styles; as a graphic artist he has been responsible for some of the most arresting book illustrations for children. With Mayakovsky he was one of the leaders of Soviet poster art in 1917–22, and was one of the few artists able to turn constructivism into a popular, hard-hitting instrument of revolutionary propaganda.

Tishler, Deineka, Pimenov and the Kukryniksi are of the younger generation. Each of them has a sharply individual style. Tishler is a romantic, one senses in his work a nostalgia for the strange. Deineka and Pimenov revel in the clean-cut forms of modern life and construction, they take a poetic delight in the filigree of girders and high tension electric cables, in the dynamics of aeroplanes, speedboats and sportsmen; Deineka particularly is instinct with the adventurous spirit of modern Soviet youth exploring not only new territories on land but a new social world. The Kukryniksi, nurtured on the culture of the great Russian satirists and on the revolutionary art of Daumier, have brought an atmosphere of great maturity as well as vitality to Soviet art. And to-day there is a still younger generation of Soviet realists with great individuality crowding to the fore; such artists as Pakhomov, Samokhvalov, Shmarinov.

Sculptors of course work under much the same conditions. They too have their section of the Workers of Art Union (RABIS), special departments in other artists' organisations such as the Artists' Clubs, the Artists' Creative Union (the MOSSKh), and in the Committee for Art Affairs. Leading sculptors are now teaching in the schools and very adequately coping with a great deal of sculptural work that has increased to-day because of the enormous demand for sculptoral decoration in the new cities, in the liberated cities and for war memorials. There are over 200 members of the Russian sculptors' section of the Co-operative. They too are eligible for commissions, contracts and *"kommandirovki"* on the same basis as the artists. There are large numbers of contracts for the modelling of small figures and figurines for domestic decoration. But most of the sculptors' work to-day is in the form of direct commissions (usually negotiated through the Co-operative) for monumental work.

The Moscow Underground railway has already ordered many scores of figures, groups and bas-reliefs for its stations. Sculpture for the projected Palace of Soviets will take many years to complete. The architects' studios that are in charge of the reconstruction of Moscow and other cities all have consultant sculptors, such as Mukhina, Chaikov, Merkurov, Manizer, Shadr, whose studios are working to full capacity.

What are the main difficulties that still face the Soviet artist? Firstly, I think that painting is handicapped because the schools are still only now recovering from the former dominance of the "Left" with its disregard of the realist tradition. On the other hand the young artist has a difficult time avoiding the wiles of easy verisimilitude offered by the strong tradition of academic naturalism. Then there is the usual battle between the artist and the still far too plentiful buyer who wants above everything to have things "just right" with the last hair on the beard of the Stakhanovite (naturalism again!). Then there is the technical difficulty that the average quality of Soviet paints still left much to be desired even in 1940. The artist also had his share of the common difficulties of the Soviet citizen in a period of rapid transition and preparation to meet the menace of Fascism. For him it expressed itself mainly in shortage of housing and studio space, lack of certain special materials, and, of course, there was the unfortunate cultural isolation that existed between the Soviets and the great Western nations at that time.

* * *

THE ARTISTS' CLUBS

When Moscow became the official centre of the Academy of Sciences as well as the seat of government, and the population jumped from 1½ to 3½ millions in ten years, living space of any description was at a premium. Some people got out of the difficulty by building pent-houses. Others went underground. Moscow artists got hold of two sets of basement-cellars and turned them into snugly equipped Masters of Arts clubs, where workers in the theatre, cinema, music, architecture and the visual arts could get together. These are the artists' social centres. The dance halls and restaurants are crowded every night; there are exhibition rooms, two miniature theatres, billiard rooms, hairdressers, all the amenities of first-class clubs.

The Masters of Arts Clubs were specially designed to bring about closer social and creative relations between the various arts, and their programmes of entertainment and other activities carry out this basic idea.

The writers, journalists and cinema people also have their special palatial clubs and there is not a night of the week the year round when something is not "on" at one or other of these centres. All the clubs naturally have a paid executive, but general policy is determined by the democratically elected Management

Councils. They are financed by the various art industries and Trade Unions.

The Government has also put the beautiful Mamontovka estate at the disposal of the Moscow artists. This is a delightful villa built by a former railway magnate on the outskirts of Moscow an historic spot, where the leading artists of the Russian 1870's used to meet. Here Serov painted his finest picture, "Girl with Peaches", and the living room in which he painted it, with all the original furniture and fittings, has been kept intact. The estate is now the property of the State and is managed by the Commissariat of Education. Applications for "passes" can be made by any member of the artistic professions and the fees are non-profit-making and very moderate, considering that a medical adviser is always on hand, diets are arranged, and the accommodation is up to the best hotel standard. I spent one of my pleasantest winter holidays there with a company of scenario writers directors, actors, actresses, painters and musicians. We talked an amazing amount of shop. Ski-ing, billiards and poker were the favourite games.

*   *   *

THE ARTISTS' CREATIVE UNION

If the Trade Unions, the Co-operatives and the Clubs are primarily designed to look after the general material well-being of the artist, the Union of Soviet Artists, described by the Russians as a "creative union", is designed primarily to cater for his spiritual welfare and the development of the arts. Each of the national areas has its Union. That of the R.S.F.S.R., the Moscow Union of Soviet Artists (MOSSKh or *Moskovski Soyuz Sovietskik Khudozhnikov*), of which I was a member, is the biggest. It is directed by an elected council of members with a paid executive. It organises lectures on art, discussions on art policy, critical debates on various schools and trends. It organises one-man exhibitions and popular public critical debates on the work of individual artists. It undertakes the study of art problems arranges exhibitions and expeditions. "The Union is a laboratory for creative discussion. It is a social centre where different creative methods and different aesthetic views are debated", writes one of its leaders. In close collaboration with the Arts and Literature Section of the Communist Academy it has undertaken important research work into the history of art and social development. Much brilliant work has been published, but unfortunately this is only now beginning to be made available in other languages. In collaboration with the various art museums it has arranged many important exhibitions: on contemporary French painting, modern English graphic art, American cartooning, modern German poster art, Chinese art—ancient and modern, and others. It has a special section for the fostering of knowledge of foreign art and has sent several artists and critics—such as Deineka, Bogorodsky and Beskin—on study trips to Western Europe and America.

When a great campaign was being organised three years ago in the art schools for a more serious and fundamental art training in anatomy and realistic technique, the MOSSKh in collaboration with the State Tretyakov Gallery organised a series of exhibitions of important Russian painters in the realist tradition— Venetsianov, Serov, Perov, Repin. A recent exhibition at the same museum collected all the best contemporary Soviet paintings illustrating the development of Socialist Realism. At the height of the discussion on the nature of Socialist Realism, the MOSSKh organised debates in which practically every artist in the capital took part.

Thanks to their extensive club life and collective organisations, Soviet artists are very closely knit as a professional group and know each other intimately. Art discussion is carried on with an intensity only rivalled by Paris in its palmiest days. These particular discussions were no exception. Reputations were torn to tatters or vindicated with equal passion. The "Left" denounced the "Photo-naturalists" as "passive observers of life, with as much creative vision as an inanimate photo-lens". The "Naturalists" replied with jeers about the lack of perception of the "Left", the few remaining Expressionists, the Cézannists, and the Formalists; they mocked at the absurdities perpetrated by those "realists" whose "ideology outstripped their knowledge of anatomy".

D

These were, then, the two extreme wings of the Soviet art world.

I remember well the debates held at the Tretyakov Gallery and the Museum of Fine Arts. The halls were crowded with painters, engravers, sculptors, critics and journalists, artists of many other professions. The proceedings opened with the chairman's speech on the subject of debate—the famous *Pravda* editorial and its lessons for the artists. In the discussion that followed trends and principles of art were attacked or defended from the standpoint of their value for the modern Soviet world of socialist construction, of their value for progress. Verbal duels, attack and repartee, were carried on in Russian fashion with the familiar form of address by Christian name and patronymic (Ivan Mikhailovich or Sergei Sergeyich) which took the sharp edge off even the most scathing invective. But there were some dramatic moments. Brodsky came down from Leningrad for a special debate on teaching. In his lapel he wore the red rosette and medal of the Order of Lenin awarded to him by the Soviet Government for his services to Soviet art; he sat in the second row and took many notes. He was regarded as the leader of the naturalists. He was even called a "photo-naturalist" and there was an apocryphal story that a photographer had once sued him for breach of copyright and plagiarism, so he was prepared to hear the Moscow artists attack his methods of work. Moscow might have been a hotbed of formalism, but it could pride itself on never falling victim to Academic naturalism.

Pointed criticism was levelled at the methods of the Academy. The evening wore on. Brodsky had his defenders, but he himself did not speak. The debate drew to an end, the chairman had already risen to sum up when the hall called for Brodsky to speak. Finally he got to his feet: "After what has already been said I doubt if anything I should say would carry weight." He spoke slowly, heavily. He had obviously been hurt by the attacks on his work. The leader of the opposition then jumped to his feet and from the floor paid handsome tribute to Brodsky's work in standing by the revolution in its darkest days, in recreating the Academy as a Soviet institution, for his painstaking and skilful

portraits of the great revolutionary leaders and pictorial recon-
structions of revolutionary scenes that had gained immense
popularity among the workers and peasants. Everyone rose to
their feet and applauded Brodsky for many minutes.

On another occasion an artist of some skill, but of mediocre
talent, came to the speaker's stand and gave a speech that was
evidently, to his mind, the acme of "correctness". He was not a
member of the Communist Party, but he gave fulsome support
to every Party line, was in full support of the *Pravda* editorial,
had always thought along those lines, etc., etc. He returned to his
place in the midst of bored silence. But when the engraver
Favorsky took his place at the stand and began with "You all
know my opinions . . ." the whole hall broke into demonstrative
applause. Favorsky, familiar in his Tolstoy blouse and flowing
white beard, was widely respected as the teacher of a score or
more of outstanding young Soviet artists and as a deeply religious
man. He never labelled himself socialist. He took the stand as a
Christian artist, a Soviet patriot. These incidents were typical of
the sincere spirit of those great debates.

These discussions were continued and developed in the
popular press and in the art journals: in *Art and Literature* (then
called *Soviet Art*), the weekly newspaper published jointly by the
State Committee for Art Affairs, the Union of Soviet Writers
and the State Committee for Cinema; in *Art*, the thick monthly
issued by the MOSSKh, and in *The Artist*, its illustrated monthly.
Shoals of letters were published in the general press. The State
Committee for Art Affairs gave the Government point of view
through its representatives at these discussions and in the press.
The Committee naturally endeavours to give a "fair field and
no favour" to every artist in his work, but it does not hesitate
to criticise drastically any tendencies that, in its opinion, run
counter to the well-being of the people and art. It was at this time
that *Pravda*, official organ of the Communist Party, published its criticism of the formalists in general and in particular
of slipshod work by Shostakovich, who is regarded as the most
talented Soviet composer. This created a great stir abroad and
was cited by the whole rag-tag and bobtail of the anti-Soviet

groups as an example of the way in which the Soviet Government was endeavouring to dragoon Russian artists and force them willy-nilly into one common mould of mediocrity. Shostakovich, they said, was doomed.

The truth is of course that the *Pravda* article said no more than several critics in other papers had said, that Shostakovich himself admitted the justice of the criticism, and on the basis of that self-criticism has subsequently gone on from success to success. The same article attacked naturalistic tendencies just as severely. I think that what shocked the "rugged individualists" abroad was that a political party should dare to pronounce an artistic judgement and put forward a clear-cut policy on art. They had evidently never read the comments on art of Marx, Lenin, Stalin or Gorky. They certainly did not understand that the Russian Communist party is, as its founders said, "a party of a new type".

These discussions on Socialist Realism occupy a unique place in Soviet art history and have had repercussions throughout the world. They were an expression of the maturing of Soviet life and art.

The 1917 Revolution was strikingly reflected in poster art, cartooning, and also graphic art, especially the woodcut. Maya-kovsky, Lebedev, Moor, Deni, Yefimov, leading graphic artists of those days, and the wood-engravers Goncharov, Kravchenko and Favorsky, have justly become world famous. But in painting and sculpture it was the vociferous artists of the left—the Futur-ists, the Suprematists and the Constructivists—who proclaimed themselves to be the only true protagonists of Revolution in art, and it was these artists who for a time succeeded in installing themselves in key positions in the art world.

On the eve of the October Revolution Russian painting was still dominated by the naturalistic painters of the Academy in Petrograd that enjoyed the patronage of the tsarist officialdom and aristocracy centred there. These painters were the official portraitists, the painters of heroic historical canvases in classical style, the preservers and glorifiers of the status quo under which they flourished or at least were favoured above other artists.

When the Revolution came all too many of these artists emigrated abroad. (Several have since returned to the Soviet Union.) The mentality of some of these artists is aptly reflected by one of their spokesmen who replied to an invitation of the Soviet government to participate in a State exhibition in 1918, with the words: "Art is for the chosen only. It cannot be the property of all."

The artistic opposition in Leningrad, the World of Art group (Mir Iskustva) that was dominated by Diaghilev of Ballet Russe fame, was by its very nature unable to give artistic direction to the turbulent and powerful social currents of the time. The World of Art was a consciously Romantic movement of aesthetes looking to the picturesque and idealised life of the past for their themes. Benois, Kustodiev, Golovin, Chekhonin, Dobuzhinsky were splendid craftsmen, but they understood nothing of the revolutionary movements of the times. And anyway their spiritual leader Diaghilev, fled from Russia with the emigrés.

The other art centre of old Russia was Moscow. This was the centre of the industrial and commercial classes, the bourgeoisie, as opposed to aristocratic Leningrad. Its art reflected its character. The revolutionary tendencies among the Russian bourgeoisie that had been manifested during the fight for the abolition of serfdom in the 1860's and that had been reflected in the socially critical and realistic art of the *Peredvizhniki* had been watered down to weakly liberal reformism in politics and to a still more weakly Cézannism in art. The Jack of Diamonds Society, in which this movement centred, ignored the robust social realities of the time and imitatively attempted to apply Cézanne's formal discoveries to the very ordinary objects of very bourgeois and middle-class studio interiors. Though individual members of all these groups "accepted the revolution", stayed on in Russia and continued to paint, sometimes like Kustodiev even attempting to show something of the October spirit and events in their work, they were neither numerous enough nor well-organised enough to take advantage of the freedom for the arts that October, 1917, brought. Thus the leadership of the painters fell into the eager hands of the *Left*, led by artists such as Tatlin the Constructivist, Malevich the Suprematist, Rodchenko, Sterenberg and others. These artists could be described as "revolutionary formalists". They were opposed to "illusionary representation" in painting. The camera, they said, could do that sort of thing much better than the painter. They therefore sought to banish the study of anatomy from the art schools as the artist had no need of this knowledge in his search for significant abstract forms. They denounced asel painting. According to them it was a concession to bourgeois individualism, for art belonged wholly to the masses, to the streets, the squares and public buildings. The *Left* were particularly incensed by the staid old-fashioned art of provincial Russia, with its sentimental bowls of flowers, sylvan glades at twilight and so on. They denounced the stale formulas by means of which the Academicians churned out pictures.

But in banning pictorial representation of reality from painting, they were in effect pauperizing art by depriving it of one of its major sources of inspiration and effect.

The *Left* were iconoclasts. But they said that they stood for a scientific, constructive art. Art must be a science, an industry. Pictures and sculptures should be constructed according to exact scientific principles after colours and forms had been classified according to their human reaction values. This might take some time to do, but when it had been done there would be no more art—there would be the higher scientific activity of designing effective constructions in colour or abstract forms, just as to-day chairs and tables, houses and machines are designed to fulfil their purely utilitarian functions in the most economic and efficient way. A picture according to the *Left* was really nothing but a "machine" for generating certain predetermined human reactions. Artists should be engineers of form and colour. The *Left* called their studios "workshops". In the *Proletcult* theatre and at the *Meyerhold* the *Left* actors wore *acting overalls* in place of costumes. It was under their influence that the Moscow Art school came to be called the VKhUTEMAS—the Higher Art-Technical Workshops. For the *Left*, beauty was a bourgeois superstition.

Foreign visitors to Russia at that time—1917–24—were rightly amazed at some of the manifestations of this art. There was, for example, Tatlin's design for a monument to the Third International: a steel mast-like structure surrounded by three concentric spirals revolving at different speeds. Malevich's pictures were built up of rectangles of separate colours and looked like patiently executed crazy quilts. A typical Rodchenko canvas, which can still be seen in the Leningrad Russian Museum, consists of a white canvas with a large black square painted on it—but the black square is not quite square.

Such extreme, formalistic views on art are of course a thing of the past to-day. There is no doubt that they were in the long run a negative influence on the development of Soviet art, but they also made a positive contribution. Their fearless, though only too often intemperate criticism cleared the air for a re-appreciation of artistic values. They took the artists out of the snobbish "world of Art", out of the cloud-cuckoo-land of "art for art's sake" and set him alongside the designers, the engineers, the workers and the rank-and-file revolutionaries who were doing the practical job of demolishing the old ramshackle tsarism and building up a new world.

It was a natural step for these *Left* artists finally to leave "pure" art and take to the industrial arts. As Gan, one of their theoreticians expressed it: "Art is done for. There is no place for art in a society of Labour, Technique, Organisation." Many of the most talented members of the *Left* then turned their attention to industrial art and design, the cinema, theatre and the decoration of public festivals and buildings. Rodchenko became one of the Soviet's most original book-designers and is an outstanding cameraman. Tatlin's work greatly influenced industrial design. Malevich went in for pottery and textile design. Sergei Eisenstein became one of the greatest masters of the screen. Lebedev of Leningrad and Mayakovsky, poet and artist, opened a whole new field in poster design: the famous Rosta Windows. These were stencilled posters made at great speed and with poetic captions dealing with the last-minute news from the revolutionary fronts. They were made at the Russian Telegraph Agency (forerunners of Tass) offices and put up in Agency windows in Moscow and other centres. This type of poster has been resuscitated in the present war with the same enormous success as before.

This voluntary departure of the *Left* artists from the field of the fine arts, brought its influence there gradually to an end.

Their ideas of the role of art in a socialist society undoubtedly stemmed from the fact that many of the bourgeois intellectuals who supported the revolution against tsarism, conceived the "dictatorship of the proletariat" to be some sort of Wellsian technocracy. The development of Soviet life itself disproved their contentions and by 1924 their ideas were pretty thoroughly discredited. New influences were at work in the schools and artists' societies. Between 1924 and 1930 there were fierce disputes between the various groups.

There was first the AKhR (Association of Artists of the Revolution). It called on the artists to place their art at the service of the revolution, to glorify its history and achievements in pictures and sculpture. This was one of the largest of the new groups, it attracted most of the artists who were good naturalistic pictorial illustrators, many of the Academicians like Isaac Brodsky, Katzman, Sokolov-Skalya. The last is to-day head of the new Tass Window studios and one of the best of the "historical genre" painters. The OCTOBER society was the successor to the *Left* and sought to unite all artists, painters as well as industrial designers into one group with the primacy in the hands of the industrial designers. The OST (Society of Easel Painters) maintained a demand for the separate existence of painters and the protection of easel painting from the attacks of the *Left*. It sought to show that easel painting, which had achieved such an enormous development in capitalist bourgeois society, also had a role to play in socialist society. In addition there were numerous other more specialised groups such as the "Four Arts", the "Red Rose" (a group of expressionists in Leningrad), The Society of Landscape Painters and so on. One artist might belong to two or even more societies. All the societies affirmed their desire to assist in the great work of building socialism, though they differed as to the best way to do this.

Meanwhile the country as a whole was settling down to the

GENERAL VIEW OF ROMODAN STATION

A 1933 "Pravda" cartoon by the Kukryniksi

(Indian ink)

ILLUSTRATION TO "THE MARRIAGE" BY GOGOL

(Indian ink)   *by the Kukrynil*

TWO COLLECTIVE FARM MEMBERS

(Oil painting)   *by Alexander Samokhvalov*

64

THE HITLER HORDE

(Charcoal) *by Dmitri Shmarinov*

THE PLUNDER ARMY

(Charcoal) *by Dmitri Shmarinov*

period of economic restoration and reconstruction after the stormy years of the revolution, civil war and intervention. Socialism gained its great economic victories after its earlier political and military victories. It became definitely the dominant tendency in all branches of Soviet life. The Soviet public looked to the arts to find affirmation, inspiration and encouragement for the great creative tasks that they had set out to solve. The public were no longer either stimulated or amused by the theoretical wrangles of the ultra-left *Left* that had created such considerable confusion of method in the schools.

A new generation of Soviet educated students entered the art schools. Many of them were Communists back from the fronts, politically and socially mature. More were Young Communist League members, new intellectuals from the factory benches. They wanted to reflect and foster the spirit of the country, the life that they knew and loved, the life that they were trying to build as Soviet citizens and voters. They wanted the tools of art for this job. The stage was set for a rebirth of realism, but in the schools and societies they found that the formalists and their methods were unable to provide them with the tools. The formalists had banished the study of anatomy, and these new young artists were above all else interested in Man. They found that the naturalists and the Academicians were so lost in a maze of detail or in their interest in superficial surface effects that they could not elucidate or project the basic features of phenomena in telling artistic form. They found the old Jack of Diamonds artists still in wrapt contemplation of studio goldfish, and nature-morte, and "views from my studio window" while industrial giants were being raised up at Dnieprostroi or the Kuzbas and the Bolsheviks were moving mountains in Magnitogorsk. However the best of the older generation of realist artists were re-entering the schools as teachers. Favorsky, Kupreanov, Ryazh-sky, Sergei Gerasimov and Johanson became the outstanding influences in Moscow painting. Petrov-Vodkin, Brodsky and Lebedev were the teachers in Leningrad. Most of the finest of the present generation of young Soviet artists have been taught by them. Favorsky trained Deineka and Pimenov, the painters, as well as Pikov, Goncharov, Echeistov and half a dozen other outstanding wood-cut artists. Kupreanov trained the Kukryniksi and Kanevsky. Lebedev trained Pakhomov and Charushin, the finest childrens' illustrator and animal artist in the Union. Sergei Gerasimov trained Boyim, Rodionov, Dekhterev and Shmarinov, three of the finest lithograph and charcoal illustrators. The latter recently won one of the coveted Stalin Prizes for his work. Samokhvalov was a pupil of Petrov-Vodkin.

It was at this time (1927) that the first really significant works of Soviet painting and sculpture were created: Petrov-Vodkin's "Death of a Commissar", Deineka's "Defence of Petrograd", Sokolov-Skalya's "People and Years", pictures by Pimenov, Williams, Nissky, Gerasimov and sculpture by Vera Mukhina, Shadr, Somova, Korolyev and others. The graphic arts, cartoons, posters and woodcuts had achieved a realist contemporary quality from the very first days of the revolution. In the person of these young artists, painting too began to show a truly contemporary modern character, and it was as obvious to the artists as it was to the public, that the path of its development lay in the study and fostering of the realistic trend.

It was in this situation that the artists, the Government and the Communist Party reviewed the whole position of art and art training. The discussion and debates on socialist realism were part of this popular review of the role and direction of Soviet art. As a result of these discussions the government set up its Committee for Art Affairs, which is the nearest thing to a real Ministry for Art that any modern government possesses. There was no doubt that the Committee was urgently needed to free the arts from the harmful influence of the "ultra-*Left*" formalists who had, to the detriment of the schools, hindered the development of sound tuition in the realist tradition. At the same time it was necessary to expose the pretensions of the Naturalists. The Committee for Art Affairs was also given the task of creating unions of artists, based on the broad programme of Socialist Realism, which would put an end to the wrangles of the numerous little sects and societies like the AKhR, the October Group, OST, OMKh, etc. and thus prepare the artists organisationally for the part they were to play in the building of socialism and later in the supreme struggle against fascist invasion. This is how the Creative Unions of Soviet Artists were initiated, and preparations made for the calling of an All-Union Congress of artists.

The State Committee for Art Affairs is to-day a body appointed directly by the Council of People's Commissars, which is the Soviet equivalent to the British Cabinet. Its head is not a member of the Council but he is of course in constant touch with the Council and is the Council expert on all matters of art policy. He is in actual control of the budget appropriations for art. He supervises all the theatres, museums, art schools and appoints their directors. He has the final say in the organisation of the great art festivals and government-sponsored exhibitions. He is adviser to the commissariats and officials responsible for specialised art training in various branches of industry. The formerly existing arts section of the Commissariat of Education was thus superseded in its general function, but it was retained to supervise art training in the general schools system on the lines laid down by the Committee for Art Affairs. A separate section of the Arts Committee deals with all cinema affairs and there is now another section for architecture.

Kerzhentsev, a critic and writer, was appointed to be the first Chairman of the Arts Committee. His job was to tend the arts, to give impetus or direction wherever needed, and act as government spokesman on art and art policy. The present holder of the post is Khrapchenko.

All the artist's Trade Unions, Clubs and Co-operatives are based on the elective democratic principle. The lower branch organisations meet frequently—weekly or monthly—for routine business. Most of these posts are filled by voluntary unpaid workers who regard this as their 'social work'. Regional or district conferences are held at longer intervals to decide how to implement the wide policies laid down at annual Republican or All Union conferences. The bigger organisations elect standing committees to direct affairs between general meetings. The central offices of course employ staffs of paid executives. In the artists' Co-operative, the elected Central Council is assisted by the heads of the executive and business staff who manage the co-op studios, shops, workshops, potteries and exhibition galleries. All decisions relating to contracts and travelling commissions are approved by a committee of artists, critics and business personnel elected yearly by the annual general conference of co-operative members. The MOSSKh is also directed by an elected council.

The artists develop contacts with art circles abroad either directly or through the medium of the All-Union Society for Cultural Relations with Foreign Countries (VOKS).

The Soviet artist has the two-way control of state policy in his particular field that is characteristic of all Soviet productive life. As an artist he can instruct his local representative to the All-Union Supreme Soviet (in English terms: his member of the Soviet parliament) and advise him of his wishes for transmission to the government and the Arts Committee. As an artist in his Trade Union, creative union, co-operative or place of work, he controls or revises in a positive direction the local application of the art policy and plans adopted by his government. And there are of course other channels through which he can exercise his right of initiative or criticism. He can for example take up any particular art question with one of the several Soviet artists who are also members of the Supreme Soviet, such as Alexei Tolstoy, or Moskvin the actor, or Barsova the actress, or Korneichuk the Ukrainian writer, who will always lend an attentive and expert ear. He can approach the Arts Committee or the Government directly, or raise his particular problem in the press.

Very large numbers of Soviet artists and critics are members of the Communist Party or Young Communist League, and they naturally also take an active part in shaping the Party policy on art.

IV

SOVIET ART POLICY

"An art that is national in form, and socialist in content."—J. V. STALIN.

★

UNLIKE most governments, the Soviet government has a policy for artists; it gives them the same security of livelihood and scope for productive work that is the right of all citizens of the state. But the Soviet Government also has a policy for art. This has caused some misgivings in conservative, liberal and even in socialist circles abroad. The gist of these criticisms is that it is perfectly all right for governments to have powers over education, national health and life or death, but that art should be "free", that a government with an art policy is almost inevitably bound to limit the creative freedom of the artist, and that civil servants with power over art are certain to want to put rubber stamps of approval or disapproval on paintings and poems. In a word, that a government with an art policy is bound to increase the censorship over art.

In the West we have had several unfortunate experiences of civil service art censorship. For instance when New York customs officials demanded the payment of duties on a famous Brancusi abstract sculpture because it was not art but "just brass". The English countryside is littered with terrible examples of "Mayor and Corporation" art. It is not forgotten of course that private patronage of art is also no guarantee against stylistic or ideological interference with the artist. An example of this was the destruction of the Diego Rivera mural in the Rockefeller Centre, New York. And then there is the wholesale prostitution of art in Nazi Germany.

Soviet art policy to-day certainly improves the material position of artists. It spreads the enjoyment of art. Is it likely to improve the artists' position in this matter of creative freedom?

Will it, as its supporters contend, foster the deeper development of art?

As summed up by Stalin, Soviet art policy aims at the creation of an art that is national in form and socialist in content. I met only one artist in the U.S.S.R. out of scores of personal acquaintances, who expressed disagreement with that aim. But he was also anti-semitic, pro-capitalist, an avowed "individualist" who hated Bolsheviks. And that was in 1935. Living experience— the incomparable opportunities that the Soviets gave him for developing his beloved folk art—proved more convincing than prejudiced theory, however, and the last I heard of him was that after many vicissitudes he was in the running for a decoration for his work in developing folk art. The Soviet Government's art policy, like the socialist policy of the government as a whole, has the overwhelming support of the people. Art, from the government's point of view, is a means capable of powerfully contributing toward development of a new socialist human being, a type of man who instinctively couples public and private well-being in his mind, who does not, like Colonel Blimp, act as if his own private welfare were necessarily the same as that of the public, but who consciously seeks the common good. The conscious aim of Soviet art is to mould the mentality of a really well developed citizen of the world and fit him for life under the most modern conditions. Soviet art therefore, to fulfil its function, must be instinct with the spirit of socialism. It must be "socialist in content."

It was the maturing of Soviet life in the 1930's that made this demand for a socialist realist art a conscious social demand on the part of the soviet public. The U.S.S.R. was transformed economically, politically and socially in the twelve years from 1928 to 1940. It became one of the four greatest industrial and agricultural powers of the world. These economic successes were accompanied by a steadily rising standard of living, universal social security, the elimination of unemployment. The Soviet Union became a socialist society of workers, collective farmers and intellectuals, collective owners of State property, a democratic socialist State conscious of its power and dignity.

Just as the maturing bourgeois society of France in the 1830's evoked the bourgeois realism of Courbet and Daumier, so the new socialist generation of the U.S.S.R. presented the "social demand" for a socialist realist art.

Why should such an art be realistic? The Soviet artist maintains that socialist thought is based on the philosphy of dialectical materialism. This philosophy enables man to achieve an understanding of things that is a closer approximation to ever-changing reality than was ever before possible. The vast increase of scientific knowledge that this makes possible enables man to control historical development in a way that was previously impossible. Socialist ideology therefore is realist and creative in the deepest sense. Its artistic expression therefore cannot but be realistic.[1]

Socialist realism is thus a higher development of the bourgeois realism of the 14th to 20th centuries in Europe. It is the natural successor of the great realist tradition of such artists as Giotto, Michelangelo, Rembrandt, Daumier, and of the English Constable and Hogarth. At the point where typically bourgeois art descends step by step from the truest vision of reality that it attained, and *dis-integrates* in the realms of phantasy, in Cubism, Constructivism, Expressionism, and sur-realism, it is there that Socialist

[1] The truth of this Marxist contention cannot be discussed at length in this book. The Soviet point of view is well expressed in Stalin's *Leninism*, from which the following quotation is taken: "Materialism recognizes objectively real being (matter) as independent of consciousness, sensation, experience . . . consciousness is only the reflection of being, at best, an approximately true (adequate, ideally exact) reflection of it." (Lenin. *Selected Works*, Vol. XI., p. 377.) Stalin himself adds: "Marxist philosophical materialism holds that the world and its laws are fully knowable, that our knowledge of the laws of nature, tested by experiment and practice, is authentic knowledge having the validity of objective truth, and that there are no things in the world which are unknowable, but only things which are still not known, but will be disclosed and made known by the efforts of science and practice." And finally: "The strength and vitality of Marxism-Leninism is derived from the fact that it relies on an advanced theory (historical materialism) which correctly reflects the needs of development of the material life of society and that it deems it its duty to utilize every ounce of the mobilizing, organizing and transforming power of its theory" (i.e., in art, science as well as politics, economics. J.C.).

ideology and its art bound up with the great progressive labour movement carries human vision forward again to Realism, *re-integrates* it, and advances to Socialist Realism, to a truer vision of the world and to yet greater heights of art and humanist inspiration. It enables the artist to depict reality accurately in its revolutionary development.

In 1917, it was not clear what the art style of the socialist Soviet society would be. All sorts of Constructivist and Expressionist "art rebels" described themselves, as we have seen, as the "only true proletarian artists". But by the 1930's it was already clear that the art style of Soviet socialism must be Realistic. Its general characteristics were emerging. It was clear that the predominant part of Soviet artists were utilising creatively the visual three-dimensional appearance of objects. True, they also utilised flat or decorative forms, but this is not a dominant characteristic. It is also clear that the successful development of Socialist art demands a deep knowledge of all the great advances that visual art has made through the centuries, and that its creator must be imbued with a deep consciousness of Socialist Humanism.

Socialist Realism is only now in process of recognisable evolution. Many elements, many influences are taking part in its development. I mentioned a few of its historical sources. In the Soviet Union, the evolution of the style is in the hands of young men like Deineka, the Kukryniksi, Gerasimov, Pakhomov, Samokhvalov.

While the historian or critic of Renaissance times could not foretell the many variations in Renaissance style that would be introduced by great artists, he certainly knew that the general development of Renaissance art would be Realist and Humanist, and, if he supported the Renaissance, he would, like da Vinci, urge its principles, not only by example, but by precept. In the same way we also know the general direction of development of Socialist Realism, though we do not know in detail how any particular theme will be treated.

Socialist Realism, says the Soviet artist, is not a style of painting that, like so many modern modes, can be put on or sloughed off with the facility of a masquerade costume. It demands a stern process of self-training in the present generation of artists, most of whom were schooled in the old society. It will be easier for the next generation. It cannot be arrived at purely by studio experiments, though such experiments are as necessary in art as in scientific progress. The Socialist Realist must go out and seek a living contact with the progressive movements of mankind. He must not only understand the sources and aims of the New World, he must feel its emotional stimuli. The Socialist Realist must be a philosopher, a dialectician, a statesman and a craftsman. He must not only be inspired by the great forward surge of mankind to-day. He must himself be a source of its inspiration.

Stalin, at the interview with a group of writers at which he initiated the phrase Socialist Realism, added: "Write the truth. Nothing in nature can be understood if it is taken in an isolated form, apart from its relation with surrounding phenomena, apart from its movement, its change, its development. . ."

To write the truth means to see the leading, dominant characteristics in any given phenomenon. Zhdanov, leader of Leningrad throughout the heroic days of the siege, developed this theme further: "Stalin calls writers, 'engineers of the human soul'. What does this mean? It means that they must know life in order to represent it, not scholastically, not as 'still life', not simply as 'objective reality' (naturalistically, J. C.) but in its real, revolutionary development. At the same time, truth and historical concreteness in artistic representation must be combined with the purpose of encompassing the ideological transformation and re-education of the working people in the spirit of Socialism."

In this broad sense Socialist Realist art is "propagandist". But in this sense it is no more nor less propagandist than all of the finest art of Western civilisation that has been based fundamentally on the Humanist and Christian ideology that inspired the Renaissance. The call for socialist realism has mobilised the widest circles of Soviet artists. It is a policy put forward by Soviet artists as members of the democracy. Mayakovsky, the poet, speaking for Soviet artists, writes:

E

I don't want to be
                    a wayside flower,
plucked after work
                    in an idle hour.
I want Gosplan
                    to sweat in debate
assigning my output
                    as part of the state.
I want the pen
                    to equal the gun,
to be listed
                    with iron
                              in industry.
And the Polit Bureau's agenda:
                    Item One,
To be Stalin's report on
                    "The Output of Poetry."[1]

But Stalin, the statesman, writes: "He (the writer) must not be obliged to write about collective farms or Magnitogorsk. Such things cannot be written about by command."

Mayakovsky is hailed by Stalin as "the greatest poet of our Socialist epoch". Soviet art has not yet produced a genius in the field of painting comparable to Mayakovsky, whose stature grows with the years. But a galaxy of young artists has carried forward Russian art from the essentially bourgeois Romanticism of Levitan, the bourgeois Realism of Serov, Repin, Surikov and other "Peredvizhniki", through the "Sturm and Drang" period of Constructivism, Suprematism, Expressionism, and on to the foothills of Socialist Realism—the expression of their epoch. Compare the work of Deineka: The *Bathers, Physical-culture Defence of Petrograd;* the work of the Kukryniksi, *The Face of the Counter-Revolution;* The *Collective Farm Women* and *Rab-Fa. Student,* of Samokhvalov, the latter's *Metro-Stroi Workers;* the wood-cuts of Staronosov on *Lenin;* the sculptures of Mukhina—

[1] Translation by Herbert Marshall. Published in *Mayakovsky and His Poetry* in this series, by Pilot Press.

compare these representative creations of Soviet art with the
work of the older artists.

An entirely new type of artist is developing, whose themes are
Socialist, whose style is . . . how else describe it? . . . the Realism
of Socialist Humanism.

Deineka's studio is filled with light. He himself can be found
at the aerodromes, with the parachute jumpers, with the Black
Sea Fleet in the sunny Crimea, with the tractor drivers of the
collective farms and large scale machine-tractor stations, with
the sportsmen, in the mines, at the front. The Kukryniksi are
staff artists for Pravda. They go on probing satirical visits
to pinion bureaucrats on the railways and offices; they are specially
assigned by Stalin to illustrate the events of the History of the
Revolution and Civil War; in their summer holidays they used
often to separate: one to the vineyards of the Caucasus, one to the
factories of the Urals and the third to the Crimean resorts. I
once telephoned the young artist Dorokhov for an appointment.
"I am afraid that I shall be busy tomorrow" he said. "I am
flying to the Donbas. I have an assignment to do three portraits
of Stakhanovites." These young artists cannot imagine the
creation of art without this close contact with modern life.

This getting out into the new life was particularly important
for the older generation of artists. Many of them had been
brought up to think that there was something ugly about in-
dustrialisation, that they could best fulfil their purpose by
commemorating the quiet beauty of flowers and country scenes.
For them it was a difficult break with the past to realise the
romanticism of industry, the heroism of industrial achievement,
to understand the high calling of the artist who could bring home
the beauty of the new life to the young Soviet generation and
who could help to condition the mind and emotions of the
peasant to the modern industry and agriculture of socialism. For
this reason special facilities are offered to enable the artist to
travel about the country and get to know its peoples. There are
numerous scholarships, "creative assignments" and posts with
exploration and scientific groups. Workers' and collective
farmers' clubs make a practice of inviting artists to visit them

and show them their work, and in their turn they take the greatest delight in acquainting the artists with their life and work. It is not expected of course that you can turn an artist into a Socialist Realist or a "proletarian artist" simply by getting him to visit or work in a factory, nor is it expected that an artist will immediately become a sort of proletarian Michelangelo as soon as he starts painting factories or revolutionary demonstrations instead of sylvan glades and apples and studio nudes, but experience has shown that when an artist himself consciously approaches new revolutionary or socialist subject matter in a spirit of sincerity, he is able to change his own artistic nature. For the average artist who has been brought up under the old regime, this is no easy task. But, for the younger generation, intimate and creative contact with the new world of Socialism cannot but strengthen the vital elements in its art. On the other hand self-isolation from the new life can only lead to premature sterility. Within the Soviet Union, the ideological expression of capitalism in art is not merely retrograde, but reactionary. The artist who rests obsessed with the negative elements constituted by the vestiges of capitalism in the socialist state is a cultural drag. The path of creation can only lie forward, and forward it can only go with the socialist proletariat and peasantry, towards the classless society of the people.

For those painters who have been nurtured by the Soviets from early youth, this creative identification with the people comes naturally, as a matter of course. For the older generation of artists, particularly in the early days of the Soviets, it had to come about as a conscious effort of will based on an understanding of the inevitable course of history. The Soviet art policy is to make this transition as easy and complete as possible by education and by placing all possible facilities at the disposal of the artists.

*　　　*　　　*

The second part of Stalin's well known slogan, calls for an art that is national in form. It is often asked, why should the Soviets strive to foster various national arts when their ideal is an international society in which national barriers have been done away with? The Soviet answer to this is simple: in the world in general, and in the Soviet Union in particular, the people speak in a myriad tongues. There are 182 different peoples in the U.S.S.R. alone. Each has its own deep-rooted traditions of artistic imagery and symbols which stir its emotions and imaginations with peculiar force. If the new ideas are to be most deeply effective, then, isn't it most practical for them to be expressed in the art language of each people, be it Russian, Tartar or Uzbek? Discussing this question Stalin declared that the Bolsheviks did indeed support the future evolution of national cultures into one general culture with one general language, but at the same time they support the growth of national culture at the present period of Soviet development. "Now", he said, "there is nothing strange in this. National culture must be allowed to develop and expand, developing all its potentialities in order to create the conditions for their evolution into one general culture with one general language—that is the direct dialectic Leninist way of putting the question of national cultures."

These reasons alone would be sufficient explanation of the way in which the Soviets encourage the national idiom in all the arts. One of the reasons why opera is so popular in Russia is that, not only is there a rich fund of Russian operas, but foreign operas are translated into Russian, and by skilful production they are made as comprehensible as possible to the audience. Shakespeare too has been very fully translated, and some theatres have not hesitated to adapt his stage directions in order to make them still more accessible to the Russian audience. For instance the Revolutionary Theatre's production of *Romeo and Juliet* brought out the essentially poisonous nature of the feud between the two noble houses in a most effective way by showing the natural friendliness existing between the common retainers of the nobles. One may ask where is the Socialism in these examples, but it must be remembered that socialist culture aims at the critical assimilation of the finest in the art of the ages. As Lenin wrote: "Proletarian culture is not something that has sprung nobody knows whence, it is not an invention of those who call themselves experts in proletarian culture. That is all nonsense. Proletarian culture must be the result of a natural development of all the stores of knowledge which mankind has accumulated under the yoke of capitalist society, landlord society and bureaucratic society."

Here is another example of this popularisation of the arts by translating them into national idiom. It was found that some peasants had great difficulty in getting the hang of Beethoven's symphonies in full orchestration, so the Union of Soviet Composers prepared a special score for the balalaika, the popular Russian peasant guitar. By this means the peasants' ears were prepared for the rich tonalities of Beethoven's orchestration. And here is a more practical example: when the Five-Year Plans were launched, the main slogans of work were devised by the Central Committee of the Soviets in Moscow, but it was the artists in each of the national republics who put these slogans into locally popular poster form.

The freedom of national cultures that the Soviets have brought about as part of their national policy has resulted in the most amazing richness and diversity of art forms. The arts of the Central Asian Republics in particular have been reborn in a glory that they only knew in their most ancient days. One of the most stimulating features of Soviet art life is the extensive interchange of art between the various republics. This is specially fostered by the Committees for Arts. Each year, festivals of national arts are organised in the various capitals, and these have been continued even in the midst of war. None of the ancient countries of the East, with the exception of China, has seen such a modern renaissance of national culture as Soviet Uzbekistan, Kazakhstan, or Buryat-Mongolia. There is no doubt that the fertilising forces of development have been national freedom and Socialism.

Soviet art policy is determined and put into operation in exactly the same way as other policies of the democracy: that is, by democratically controlled analysis of the situation and democratically determined action. This of course does not obviate the responsibilities of leadership. The Government is elected to give that leadership. It was in response to the demands of the situation that the Government created its Committee for Art Affairs in 1932, to carry out the policy of achieving an art that is "Socialist in content, national in form." It was in close collaboration with the artists organisations that the widespread organisational measures needed, were carried through. It was not to be avoided that some reputations should suffer during these changes, or that some sensibilities should be hurt in the frank discussions which accompanied them. But when one surveys the magnificent achievements of the Soviet Theatre, the Cinema, literature, music, song, architecture and folk art in its widest sense, or the way that the Soviet spirit has stood up to the Nazi attack, one cannot doubt the correctness of Soviet art policy. Certain it is that under that policy the status of the Soviet artist and art has been immeasurably enhanced. In the directives given by the Government and stressed by Stalin for the carrying out of that art policy it was explicitly stated that the old idea of intellectuals as "fellow-travellers" of the Revolution was no longer applicable to the Soviet intellectuals "who must be treated with respect and care in the name of the well being of the workers and peasants."—(ISKUSTVO, NO. 6, 1939).

Stalin, Zhdanov and other Soviet leaders have given the artists outstanding assistance in developing their organisations and their art. This has not been limited to general measures of economy and direction, general policies, but in numerous cases has included personal and direct contact and advice. Soviet politicians take direct responsibility for art policies, but because their political philosophy is a universal and humanist one, they are able to approach these problems in the spirit of the artist.

No description of the evolution of Soviet art policy would be complete without tribute to the enormous role played by Maxim Gorky in its development. As the close friend and collaborator of Stalin, and as leader of the Soviet writers, he was a leading influence in the trend to socialist realism. He was of course mainly interested in its literary manifestations, but he took a direct interest in the graphic arts too. In 1933, for instance, the Kukryniksi were commissioned to illustrate his book *Klim Samgin*. They completed fifty drawings and sent them to him for approval.

Gorky turned down forty-seven, and invited them to dinner. He gave them an analysis of his novel, he discussed the drawings in detail. The Kukryniksi went home, re-read the novel and turned out illustrations as incisive as the book itself. This exercise in intense realism has reflected itself in all their succeeding work, particularly the illustrations to Gogol's *Dead Souls* which are the finest of the kind. As a result of the work of the Kukryniksi, Sergei Gerasimov, Dekhterev, Shmarinov, Samokhvalov and others, Soviet illustration to-day holds a leading place, if not the leading place, in that art to-day, and the great Russian satirists have at last found illustrators worthy of their mettle.

AN INCONVENIENT CUT AT A BUCHAREST TAILORS

Cartoon by Ganf.

"You've completely spoiled this uniform! I can't raise my arms in it!

THE EXECUTION OF ZOYA KOSMODEMYANSKAYA

(Oil painting)

by the Kukryniksi

"THE CAPTURE OF KOKENHAUSEN FORTRESS BY IVAN THE TERRIBLE
(Oil painting)   *by Pavel Sokolov-Skaly*

IVAN INSPECTS THE FIRST PRINTED RUSSIAN BOOK
(Oil painting)   *by Pavel Sokolov-Skaly*

SHCHUS, COMPANION-IN-ARMS OF THE ANARCHIST
BANDIT MAKHNO

(Water colour and ink)   *by the Kukryniksi*

THE SHOWER BATH

V

ART FOR, AND OF, THE PEOPLE

Citizens of the U.S.S.R. have the right to rest and leisure . . . and education.—THE SOVIET CONSTITUTION.

★

I LIVED and worked in the U.S.S.R. throughout the whole immense effort of the First Five Year Plan. I saw the people work as if inspired and put up stoically with greater hardships of everyday life than we in Britain have yet seen in this war, if the Nazi air blitz is excepted. But as a result of that enormous effort the U.S.S.R. transformed itself into a rich socialist democracy that could afford to assure all its citizens the right to work, to rest, to leisure and education.

I remember well the excited discussions that followed Molotov's announcement that the U.S.S.R. was now in truth a socialist society. Some of the foreign correspondents were sceptical. "Where's the equality?" they asked. "There are still rich Russians and poor Russians too." This was true in a sense. Some skilled workers, writers and engineers were relatively wealthy. Many people still just managed on their incomes, though there was a basic adequate "social security" level for all. But the Soviet leaders pointed out that "by equality, Marxism means, not equalization of individual requirements and individual life, but the abolition of classes . . . the equal abolition for all of private property in the means of production after they have been converted into the property of the whole of society." "Socialism entails the "equal duty of all to work according to their ability, and the equal right of all working people to receive remuneration according to the amount of work performed" (Stalin). No matter how wealthy an individual might be, or how much wealth he chose to devote to his work and personal comfort, he could never use any of that wealth to "hire" and exploit some other less fortunate human being. And of course socialism was only considered as a stage towards the development of Communism with its principle of "from each according to his ability, to each according to his needs." Further, Stalin writes: "People's tastes and requirements are not and cannot be identical, equal, in quality or quantity, either in the period of Socialism or Communism." Socialism envisages the rapid and constant raising of the technical and cultural level of manual workers to that of the most advanced mental workers. Indeed "only this can ensure the high level of productivity of labour and the abundance of articles of consumption which are necessary in order to begin the transition from Socialism to Communism." (Stalin).

This is the practical policy that lies behind the huge budget allotments for education and art in the Soviet Union even in the midst of war. Universal elementary education, the liquidation of illiteracy; free advanced study and technical training—all this has immensely extended the numbers of the cultured. And this rising standard of living and culture has gone hand in hand with the development of a truly democratic art. More good cheap books are printed in the U.S.S.R. than in any other country. More people are seeing plays in a theatre that is unrivalled in richness and variety. The U.S.S.R. has the highest comparative attendance at exhibitions and museums. And this growth is not the fortuitous product of competitive art industries scrambling for clients. It is the result of a planned, organised distribution of the cultural amenities of civilisation. Factory committees often book whole theatres for their workers. The Trade Unions take excursions to art museums as part of their regular work. In the plush and gilt Bolshoy Theatre of Opera and Ballet where the tsar¹st aristocracy used to have their hereditary boxes, there are now specially reserved seats for the shock brigaders of various factories. Exhibitions of paintings are constantly taken round the factory clubs and country clubs—these latter being cultural centres attached to the great collective farms and machine-tractor stations. In making out its yearly plan of performances, no metropolitan theatre omits to allocate a good proportion of its time to the vast provincial audience. Indeed a theatre management that neglected to take its plays out to the countryside, to the Red Army and to outlying factory centres would be sure to be censured by the Committee for Arts.

In these and many other ways, art is brought to people who before took no interest in art, because it was "above them" or "too expensive for them." It is also brought to those who, under "normal" pre-socialist conditions, found that good art was inaccessible to them, for instance, the vast populations of rural areas or what were formerly the colonial areas of the old Tsarist empire. The rising labour productivity of socialist organisation also enabled the government to cut down the hours of work. The seven-hour day was statutory in the U.S.S.R. in 1936. This naturally gave the people more leisure and inclination for cultural activities. Consumer interest in art has in these ways been systematically broadened and deepened.

In this popularising of art, the museums play a big role. They have changed radically from those of the past. They are decorated and hung so as to banish any lingering air of mustiness. Pictures are set out with their titles, names and dates of authors. They are grouped so as to show their relative position in the history of the individual artist and in the flow of social change. This has ended the museum snobbery of the "art for art's sake" fanatics who contend that a picture exists for and by itself. The Soviet method of hanging (like that so excellently devised by the National Gallery in its war-time exhibits of individual masterpieces) brings the public into direct contact with all those facts of person, time and place that add so much to a picture's significance and that the connoisseur since Vasari—and before—has always found so intriguing. The museums themselves are thus always in use and on holidays they are crowded, but in addition they have also developed a wide net of "outside exhibition" activities. They take their pictures to their audiences. In such a city as Moscow where, as a rule, several exhibitions are being held at one time, major shows are often put on at such clubs as that of the Social Service Workers or at the Railway or Metal Workers' Club. And furthermore, a wide range of popular art lectures, books, and newspaper articles keeps art constantly in the public's attention.

By these means the classic masters such as Durer, da Vinci or Rembrandt, who are well represented in the great Hermitage Museum at Leningrad, have a constantly increasing audience of appreciative admirers. But exhibitions of contemporary Soviet art are also attracting increasing attention, not least because the artists themselves are naturally re-evaluating the role of their art in relation to the people's interest. This does not mean "pandering to the popular taste." It means that the artists themselves are endeavouring to rise to the historic interests of the epoch. They have less interest in those themes that were the usual stock-in-trade of the average western artist: the intimate and personal incidents and accidents of usually humdrum bourgeois life, such as the studio interior, fleeting and usually frivolous sexual moods and the recording of the more or less accidental patterns that go to make up contemporary still life, and this fading interest in the old bourgeois themes is not due to state decrees or compulsion to "toe the Party line." It is only natural that the artist's horizon has expanded to include the widely interesting episodes of social history, the leading incidents and objects of contemporary life. New genres are being developed: what one might call the "social landscape"—the configuration of social groups. Now we are seeing landscapes treated, not only as a lyrical reflection of the artist's own spiritual experience, in the tradition of a Levitan, but in an entirely new way, as the artist's apprehension of the scene of social change and conflict, as the scene of man's greatest struggle—the conquest of nature. The Soviet artist has also become interested in new types of men; the scientist, the industrial worker, the Bolshevik as the type of working-class leader. Contrast these subjects of Soviet art with the too frequent vintage of the bourgeois Academy: the society beauty, the nude courtesan, the titled idler or politician, the romanticised "son of the soil." Just as the tender artists of our suburbs go out to study the forms and experience of the quiet countryside, so the Soviet artist goes to study the forms and experience of the factory as an essential part of his training. And naturally the interest of the Soviet artist in these new themes corresponds to the interest of the new Soviet public; the workers of farm and factory, the new intellectuals who are engrossed in the task of building a new world.

By educating the public to take a greater interest in art, and the artist to take a greater interest in the people, the Soviets have brought art to the people, and forwarded their aim of creating art for the people. As Stalin said, in a country in which there are no upper classes which could hoard or exploit art or patronise the artists, the intelligentsia, the artists, naturally take their place alongside the workers and farmers in the building up of the new socialist society. As that society has developed in the last twenty-five years, the ranks of the intelligentsia have been gradually reinforced by the new generation of Soviet intellectuals, who are themselves of the people, who have been wholly trained under the Soviets, and who therefore do not have to be won over from ingrained, preconceived "upper class" ideas about art, and life, but who, in fact, accept their oneness with the peoples as a matter of course. Thus the Soviets are realising their aim of creating an art of the people. When young workers and collective farmers join the art schools, they are taught to master and appreciate the art achievements of the past, critically, in the light of the new concepts of beauty which they themselves discover in their own life.

At the same time, Soviet Socialism is achieving greater leisure and cultural opportunity for vast numbers of people who are now finding the time and means of satisfying their inclination to participate in the creation as well as the enjoyment of art. This is not an "amateur art movement" as we have known it hitherto. It is so widespread that it can only be ranked as a specifically socialist People's Art.

In the first place, the old folk arts are carefully preserved and developed. In the R.S.F.S.R. alone there are over 200,000 registered folk artists: wood and bone carvers, rug-makers, metal workers, makers of embroidery, faience and lacquer work of exquisite beauty, notably at Palekh and Mster. In the North, in the sparsely populated home of the Chukchi, after the summer hunting season, 155 artists gather in a collective workshop-studio, and spend the arctic winter creating inimitable engravings and carvings in bone and ivory.

Every Red Army unit has its wall newspaper when in barracks or its front-line newspaper in the field. Articles, poems or drawings are never lacking. The larger units in normal times all have their club centres with art studios and workshops attached to them. The Red Army House (or Central Club for all ranks) has for many years now arranged exhibitions not only of outside art, but of Red Army art, very much as we in war time England now have our exhibitions of Civil Defence Workers' art. Red Army artists are in the main fighters who are also artists. Their art work is more than just a hobby. Similarly, every big factory club is a focal point of the workers' social life. Each has its art group which assists in dramatic productions and does most of the art work needed for the great festivals and demonstrations, for local "safety first" or production propaganda, or the wall newspapers that are so characteristic a feature of Soviet life. The big collective and State farms and the Machine Tractor Stations, centres of rural life and work, also have their clubs, courses and art circles.

In other countries the amateur artist is still regarded as merely a man with a hobby. True, in some spheres, more progressive ideas about amateur art are already producing good results and some amateur artists have built up quite important organisations for developing and distributing their art, but in the main, even in Britain and America, the amateur art movements have to wage a constant struggle for survival. In the Soviet Union the peoples' art movement is given the most serious attention by the Government and various local authorities. Large sums are expended for studio equipment. No big local government or civic centre is complete without its Palace of People's Art. 3,000 children practice art in the Pioneer Palace in Leningrad alone. The MOSSKh and the Artists' Co-operative always have dozens of portable exhibitions of original work travelling from centre to centre. The State Publishing House has a special department producing portable exhibitions of reproductions. As part of their unpaid social work, artists, both professionals and students, teach groups in the Red Army and workers' clubs. Gerasimov, Sokolov-Skalya, Yeliseyev and scores of other artists are "patrons" of schools, factories and Red Army units in which they teach or advise on matters of art.

The history of the Stalin District Art Studio of the All-Union Central Council of Trades Unions is typical of dozens of others. A group of young workers of this Moscow district took part in a local exhibition of peoples' art, and as a result of the conversations and criticism aroused, decided that they needed more systematic training in drawing and painting than they were getting in their small club circles. They then approached the District Committee of the Communist Party, and a meeting was called which was attended by the amateur painters, and representatives of the local Party, Trade Union and Soviet organisations and local factory administrations. As a result of the meeting it was decided to ask the Central Trade Union Council to furnish the funds for a central district studio where local artists could get instruction from the best painters of Moscow. The Trades Unions eventually granted a sum of 86,000 rubles for the establishment of the studio and 199,000 rubles for current expenses. Studio rooms were set aside in the Electrozavod Factory Club, one of the biggest in the district, and the artists invited as teachers included Kanevsky, one of the finest young caricaturists and satirists, Sergei Gerasimov, a popular portrait painter, Yuon, who is well known for his historical paintings, and Vera Mukhina, the sculptress who designed the figures for the Soviet Pavilion at the Paris International Exposition. The studio was formed in 1936 with an average attendance of fifty. Tuition is of course free and carried on in out-of-work hours. Some of the students have shown such promise in their work that they have been awarded scholarships enabling them to devote all their time to art. Thus the popular art movement is fostered.

The Ukrainian Government decided to hold an exhibition of Folk Art in Kiev. Representatives of the Regional Art Committees were sent out to contact all the collective farmers and co-operative artisans who drew, embroidered, modelled, carved or plied the arts in any way. They were shown fine examples of their art and advised how to improve their efforts. Wherever necessary, prospective exhibitors were supplied with materials for their work. A month or two later they were again contacted. Over 600 folk artists took part in the Kiev Regional Exhibition. Sixteen of the most talented were enrolled in the Kiev Art Institute.

The Soviet Press treats exhibitions of People's Art on a par with professional shows. New talent is constantly being discovered through these shows and competitions and, if he desires it, the amateur artist is enabled to receive the best tuition available in the art schools or special circles. As a result of one of the first of the regular Children's Art exhibitions that it organised, the Leningrad Art Academy opened the first special school for talented child artists.

The People's Art movement is even more widespread in the fields of music, theatre and literature. The Trades Unions, which are the greatest patrons of the arts after the State itself, appropriated a hundred million rubles of their 1939 budget for the service of music of the people. This was in addition to the State budget for music. In that year, 1,200,000 trade union members were studying in the music groups of Trade Union clubs. There were eighty-eight thousand farm groups, covering the Soviet countryside. So excellent is the training given in Red Army musical groups that before the war many men when they finished their service, became professional musicians. When the first All-Union Olympiad of amateur musicians was organised, ten members of the Jury Committee toured the Union, investigating the work of local music groups and giving advice. District and regional competitions were held to select the best performers for the Olympiad. All expenses connected with participation in the final and preparatory contests were paid for by the state and Trade Union organisations. As a result hundreds of thousands of musicians and singers took part in the Olympiad.

It has often been said that the Russians are natural actors. They certainly have an astonishing love for spectacle and drama. Even in Tsarist Russia there were 153 theatres throughout the country. To-day there are 825! Moscow, even in war time, is still the theatrical centre of the world. But, as in other branches of art, one of the characteristics of the new culture is that it has spread out into the great Republic and provincial centres. Important national theatres have developed in the Ukraine (99 theatres), in Uzbekistan (33 theatres), in Mongolia and Georgia, and the theatre has spread down among the people. There is not a factory or collective farm of any size that does not have its dramatic group. In the Yaroslav Region alone, there are 422 amateur dramatic groups, 237 chorus groups, 65 groups of folk dancers, 235 music circles. Thanks to the help of State or Trade Union organisations, buildings, props and other expenses are received free of charge. In the larger groups, permanent staff such as stage managers are employed and paid by the State, by the Trade Union club or local House of Culture, or by the factory to which the members of the group are attached. Professional actors, like professional artists, are only too eager to help the great new People's Theatre movement. When the Moscow Amateur Art Centre was opened in 1934, no less than 316 requests were received from noted artists, asking to be put in touch with amateur groups needing expert advisers. Their offers were snapped up, and, as a result, in 1939, a Moscow Amateur theatre festival had 56,000 participants. To-day 2,600 professional artists give voluntary service to Workers' Clubs in Moscow alone. One theatre in Moscow is devoted entirely to peoples' theatrical art, and throughout the season it plays to packed houses. Its stage is put at the disposal of dramatic groups in various big Moscow factories or districts, and these either put on occasional performances or take the theatre for a week or more. In my opinion the variety performances here were superior to the professional variety stage. They had a freshness and vitality that I have never seen surpassed on any music hall stage.

In all spheres, music, theatre, art, the People's Art movement has been an inexhaustible reservoir of talent for the professional arts.

Much has already been achieved in this movement for a real people's art, but quite obviously even more astonishing results can be expected in the future. The technical basis of the Soviet Union has been developing and expanding at a rate enabling the maintenance of a steady increase in national wealth, while the

F

work hours needed for this result have at the same time been steadily reduced. In 1934 there was a general all-round reduction to the seven-hour day. Had it not been for the urgent need to create defensive armaments against the threatened fascist attack, there would undoubtedly have been a further reduction to six, maybe even five hours within a comparatively short space of time. When in the future such a reduction is achieved—and it is by no means the limit—the Soviet citizen will then be able to have two or even more "careers", in place of the one career or job plus a part-time "hobby", that is the lot of most people to-day.

Under such conditions of course not everyone will want to devote his leisure to artistic pursuits, science will undoubtedly claim far more attention on the part of the average citizen than it does at present. But the pleasure of creating and enjoying art will be far more widespread than it is possible to imagine to-day.

The artistic *Left* in Russia once claimed that there would be no place for the professional artist in a fully developed Socialist society where all could be artists. But I hardly think they were right. Most artists will agree that the practice of art is so absorbing that a true artist will want to devote his whole time to it under any conditions.

* * *

Interesting perspectives are opened up in the Soviet Union for the development of a "synthetic" or "architectonic" type of art. In present day capitalist society, the various arts: architecture, painting, sculpture, music, the theatre, have each tended to develop along their own lines, virtually isolated from each other. The individual painter working in his studio is creating not only pictures for the people to look at, but goods to sell on the market. Economic pressure forces him to concentrate his attention on the production of goods that will sell easily: i.e., relatively small wall or easel pictures that can be easily displayed on the market on Bond Street, the Rue de la Boetie or 52nd Street, and they must be turned out so that they can be hung in either Mr. X's dining room or in Mrs. V's bedroom. The musician who writes great choral music that demands not only singers, but orchestras and dancers and a suitable auditorium, can only hope for the very rarest of performances. He therefore concentrates his attention on the individual lyric, the ballad, the symphony or concerto, etc. Hampered by all sorts of economic considerations, by private property in land, by the very lack of experience in really large-scale design, the architects of to-day think themselves lucky if they are given the job of laying out even a city block or a garden suburb. They are still waiting their opportunity to use all the great technical possibilities at their disposal to-day to design whole cities or even land areas for creative and beautiful living. Examples such as this could be multiplied, but I think that it is already clear that only a well-organised and planned society can give real opportunities for synthesising the arts again, so that they will be free not only to develop to the full their own individual and specific qualities, but also those qualities that they attain only in combination.

When great cities such as Magnitogorsk or Dnieproges are conceived from the foundations up by groups of economists, architects, social planners and designers, they can be planned as a whole. From the lay-out of the streets to the ornamental details of the lamp-posts and houses the city can be designed as a functional (productive) and artistic entity. The planners are untrammelled by "vested interests" in land or profits. Creative understanding is forged between the practitioners of various branches of art by joint work on such projects, and by association in the Masters of Art Clubs. The architect comes naturally to visualise his buildings in terms of sculptural or mural decoration, the industrial planner becomes more conscious of the workers' cultural needs and the possible contribution of the artist.

Furthermore, the great monumental buildings that a socialist cultural life demands, such as the Palaces of Culture, or the Palaces of the Soviets and other clubs, naturally demand a collaboration of all the arts. The great annual people's demonstrations and celebrations are also evolving into typically "synthetic spectacles". I remember well the Grand May Day of 1934, when the Soviets were flushed with the triumph of their Five-Ye

Plans. The whole of Moscow was decorated in festival style. Squares were set out with huge dolls and puppets, caricatures of fascists, jolly looking Ivans and Marusyas. There were fantastic artificial trees on Theatre Square and a big multicoloured spiral construction in the centre fitted with tiny mirrors reflecting a myriad lights when revolving searchlights played on them in the evening. There were gay refreshment booths and roundabouts on other open spaces. In the clear May sunshine, the crowds and marching columns of cheerful Muscovites made their way to the focus of the demonstration—the great Red Square. One side of this huge space was hung with festoons of greenery with the slogans of the International Workers' Day picked out in red bunting. On the other side the leaders of the people exchanged greetings with the people from the balconies of the russet brown Lenin Mausoleum. In the evening there were masked carnival in the Parks of Culture.

On Physical Culture Day, the Red Square is transformed into a vast arena. The granite stalls on the Kremlin side are packed to overflowing with spectators—Trade Union delegates, representatives of the Soviets, national republics, government commissars, foreign guests. On the arena space tens of thousands of splendidly built young athletes parade, march, dance and sing. Uzbek girls in their long flowing gowns and soft leather top boots; young Russians in gay sports clothes that have been specially designed for the occasion—oarsmen, cyclists and acrobats; young Tartars and Ukrainians, White Russians and Mongolians. They create an unforgettable spectacle whose name is Youth. In the great cities of the Union similar spectacles are held simultaneously, and whereas in the old days the decorations of the Red Square and others were rather makeshift, it is natural that gradually these places of spectacles that have become an essential feature of Soviet life are being gradually rebuilt the better to fulfil their function. In 1932 the Red Square cobble stones were taken up and replaced by solid granite paving stone. The wooden stands for spectators were replaced by permanent auditorium stalls. Plans are already completed for the complete rebuilding of the opposite side of the square. Similarly, the new

Moscow Palace of Soviets, whose foundations are already laid, has been planned as a place of peoples' meetings and spectacles. The massive main building profusely decorated with sculptures and frescoes will house two of the largest halls in the world, so constructed that they can be used either as auditoriums for public meetings, for theatrical performances, or for popular demonstration and spectacles. The building itself will be the focus of converging festive approaches leading to and from a vast colonnaded amphitheatre. Only in such surroundings will it be possible to produce the grand popular spectacle of Socialism, in which all the arts will be joined in a mighty hymn to the glory of man. Soviet life is resuscitating the art of the popular pageant.

VI

IN THE BATTLE AGAINST FASCISM

"The work of our artists is an organic part of the war effort and will be so regarded in the history of the patriotic war."

Izvestia (Editorial).

*

IN JULY, 1941, when fascism flung the most powerful armed force of all time against the Soviets, the nation sprang to arms and the arts donned battle-dress.

Soviet artists, like every other group of citizens, took their places in the ranks of the defence and the counter-offensive. Many exchanged the brush for the rifle. All who could answered the call for universal military training and joined the peoples militia, the A.R.P. and other war service units. Many artists in Leningrad, Moscow, Kiev, Odessa, Sevastopol—front line cities —were called on to take up arms in defence of their right to use their brushes. All put their art work at the direct service of defence. They realised the paramount necessity of smashing fascism once and for all time. This meant in the first place, direct propaganda to increase the war effort both on the front and in the production centres of the rear, but the necessary corollary was and is the need to provide normal cultural life at its highest pitch to keep the spiritual life of the Soviet people healthy.

The Soviet artists' attitude is summed up by Ilya Ehrenburg. "A writer must know how to write not only for the centuries. He should know how to write also for the one short second, in the fate of his people is to be decided in that second. . . .

"There is nothing more terrible than pseudo-wisdom, than silence for the sake of the future. History will be full of contempt for those who were silent. Let us be militant! Higher the banner! Sound the trumpet, bugler!"

As in the days of the revolution, the Civil War and Interven tion, the artists are turning out an endless stream of propaganda work. Many of them to-day, such as Moor, Yefimov, Radakov, Cheremnikh, Brodaty, Yelisayev, are veterans of those other heroic days. Many, like the Kukryniksi trio, Deineka, Gershanin, Shmarinov, Seyffertitz, Kanevsky, are newcomers trained in Soviet schools.

Nazi propaganda stakes its success on the magnitude of its lies: the bigger the lie, the greater its chance of befooling the masses. Examples of this are: the sinking of the *Ark Royal*, the "annihilation of the last Russian reserves", the "invincibility of the Wehrmacht". In the long run, however, the bigger the whopper, the bigger the cropper.

Soviet propaganda is based on the simplest exposition of the truth—as far as this is ascertainable by the best brains of the Soviet Union. That truth may be hardly discernible except to the expert. It is the job of the propagandist to make it discernible to every citizen, to make it so obvious that it is regarded as inevitable and thus create boundless confidence in the result of Soviet activities. During the long days of the Russian strategic retreat from June to December, 1941, it was the job of the propagandist to demonstrate what was known to the experts as a fact: that the Soviet come-back was inevitable and would be victorious. It was the job of the propagandist to show that this inevitability was not "a miracle", but would only come about as a result of tremendous exertions on the part of every Soviet citizen. The propagandist had to show further just what each citizen had to do to bring about the desired result. This most important task of Soviet propaganda was fulfilled with brilliant skill. Defeatism failed to obtain a grip in the U.S.S.R. even in the darkest hours, and finally the exertions of the whole Soviet population have achieved the "miracle" of hurling back the "invincible Wehrmacht" and inflicting crushing defeats on it. Truth proved to be stronger than fiction.

The democracies must weld their war unity and effort by making every citizen conscious that he has a vital role to play in his own and society's salvation. Over the whole expanse of the democratic countries, particularly in the areas far from actual fighting, the war must be brought home in all its heroism, its frightfulness and its urgency. It must be dramatized into a personal experience for tens of millions of people in the rear. It must be dramatized, analysed even for the actual combatants; its why and wherefore must be made part of every man's consciousness. Each fighter must know why he "goes over the top", even against great odds; why he must be prepared to die, if need be, so that life can be lived.

The Soviet artists know that they are engaged in a struggle for their very lives. In the occupied Soviet territories, the Nazi murderers spare neither man, woman, child nor artist or scientist. Artist or labourer, if you are caught by the Nazis, it means either death or German slavery in the literal meaning of that word. All works of art are either plundered or destroyed. There have been no exceptions to this rule in Nazi-occupied territory. Faced by these facts, inspired by the same patriotism that animates the whole Soviet people, the artists put their war effort first and their own "personal life" second. But they soon found that, when one makes the war effort paramount in such a cause as we are fighting for to-day, it soon becomes one's "personal life".

Soviet propaganda in war time is organised on the same principle as the Red Army. The "High Command" gives the general strategic aim, the local units have wide powers of initiative in the actual tactical operations. The *directives* for policy and propaganda are embodied in Government and Party statements such as Stalin's Order of the Day on the outbreak of war, where he announced the "scorched earth" policy, or in the winter of 1942 when he foretold "There will be rejoicings in our streets", and also in the short slogans that are issued from time to time. These *directives* assure that the peoples' efforts are canalised along certain channels, and that they are concentrated at the appropriate time on one or more particular objectives: "Scorch the Earth", "Remove the factories from the danger zones", "Annihilate the fascist invaders!", 'All out for Universal Military Training" "We are fighting for National Liberation".

There are several organisations engaged in spreading this propaganda. The Government itself has its press bureau: th

SovInformBureau. The Party has its Political (propaganda) Department. The Red Army maintains a great propaganda and political instruction service. The Communist League of Youth organisation with its press and its groups in every farm and factory is a channel of propaganda that touches every young person in the Union. The Trades Unions too have their propaganda sections; each Union stressing those aspects of the general line that particularly concern its members. The heavy industrial Unions stress the needs of arms manufacture, the need for women in industry; the light industrial Unions show how light industry can help the war effort by using local materials, etc. The Co-operatives, the Commissariats for Agriculture and Industry, the Trades Unions of the intellectuals: the Cinema Workers' Union, the Writers' Union, the Printers' Union, the Union of Workers of Art (actors, architects, artists)—all these in their spoken, written or poster propaganda apply the general directives to their own particular sphere, in their own particular way. Thus all the arts co-operate in the tasks of propaganda, and they reach their audiences along channels that they are familiar with through their work of peace-time propaganda in the service of the Soviets' socialist construction.

Artists are making pictures and posters for all of the organisations named above, and for many more. Many of them, like the Red Army, the TASS news agency, or the State Publishing House, employ full-time artists, but by far the greater proportion of this war time propaganda is done by the voluntary or part-time artists. (I use the phrase, "part-time" rather than "amateur" because I wish to stress the absence of "dilettantism".) The peace-time movement for the creation of a Socialist Peoples' Art has during the last ten years built up a non-professional artistic movement with a high standard of craftsmanship. Part-time artists are paid for their work at ordinary commercial rates, when they are doing professional jobs. Their social work is freely given.

Much has already been written about the Soviet wall newspapers in the peace-time struggle for the fulfilment of the Five-Year Plans. Now, they are just as essential features of war-time life in the struggle against fascism.   Every social unit: factory, farm, institute, hospital, Red Army unit, war-vessel or office has its wall newspaper that is designed and profusely illustrated by local artists. The *Lubki*, or broadsheets, originating from the days of Napoleon's defeat at Moscow, are now popularizing lampoons on Hitler or familiarising the population with the heroic deeds of Soviet patriots. These bright-coloured pictures with simple texts are extremely popular among the children and the older generation of collective farmers.

The famous *Tass* Windows are really a modernised version of these *Lubki*. They continue the tradition of the *Rosta* Windows of the days of the October Revolution. As we have noted elsewhere, the idea of them originated with Mayakovsky, poet and artist. In their present form, they are brilliantly coloured series of drawings (usually stencilled) accompanied by pungent verses. They are designed by some of the leading Soviet artists: Cheremnikh and Radlov (who worked originally with Mayakovsky), Sokolov-Skalya (present director of the *Tass* Studios), Gerasimov, Savitsky, Gershanin and the Kukryniksi. Marshak, inimitable children's poet, Kirsanov and Demyan Bedny are some of the poets who supply the texts. Two hundred artists in Moscow alone are working in these *Tass* studios, in which the lights have not been extinguished since the war began. Seven hundred issues of the *Tass* Window have gone out in thousands of copies or stencils to dozens of cities and other studio centres where they are copied or adapted. They finally appear all over the Union in different languages and, displayed in *Tass* Windows at various popular centres, they have become a feature of war-time life. Crowds collect as each new issue appears. Hundreds of suggestions for new windows come back from the public. Leningrad, Kuibishev, Tashkent, Penza, Ulan Ude, Kharkov each have their own *Tass* Window studios. The first animated cartoon *Tass* Windows are now being prepared for the screen with music by Shostakovich.

The poster technique used by Soviet artists is mainly lithographic (apart from the stencils). The vogue for photomontage seems to have passed, and the drawn or painted poster again predominates; these have been found to arouse the greatest interest among the people. Some plastic posters have also been made, part of the design being raised in semi-relief and coloured. The Art Publishing House alone has issued over 20,000,000 posters.

Very many of the artists working on contract for the Co-operative have turned their work to direct service of the war effort. This was naturally without prejudice to their contracts. The Government, the Red Army, Trades Unions, various commissariats arranged numerous commissions for artists to record the Soviet war effort, both at the battle front and on the production front. Leningrad artists Dormidontov, Samokhvalov and others, recorded every phase of the siege and liberation of the Soviets' northern capital. Sixty artists are now employed on the creation of a panorama of the defence of Leningrad. The Leningrad Union of Soviet Artists sends regular exhibits to hospitals, Red Army clubs and rest homes, and has arranged for the registration and artistic recording of all the important historical buildings of the city. Similar work was undertaken in all other threatened cities under the direction of the All-Union Committee for the Registration and Protection of Relics of Architecture and Historical Monuments (which was set up by the Committee for Arts), under the chairmanship of the veteran artist and historian Igor Grabar. This committee is charged not only with registering the destruction caused by the German invasion, but also with restoration work. Seyffertitz, working on a government commission, made some of the finest black-and-white sketches of the war during the siege of Sevastopol. He left with one of the last ships. Dorokhov, artist and Red Army man, exhibited 300 pictures at the end of 1943 in Moscow, the result of two years' work at the fronts with the Black Sea and Northern Fleets.

Moscow artists Deineka, the Kukryniksi, Pimenov and scores of others have of course been in the front line. Forty exhibitions of their war-time work were opened on May Day, 1943, in Moscow. Their work also made up a great part of the big exhibition devoted to the "Patriotic War" at the Tretyakov Gallery, Moscow, when 600 paintings were exhibited (November, 1943). Similar exhibitions were arranged in Kuibishev, Tbilisi, Yerevan,

Frunze. The sailor artists of the Baltic Fleet arranged their own exhibition of 260 paintings. Exhibitions devoted to the life of the occupied regions have a powerful stimulative effect. Opened in May, 1942, the exhibition "White Russia is and will be Soviet" showed the face of White Russia in peace time days . . . its rolling, verdant countryside, peaceful hamlets, new factories and towns of the Five-Year Plans and then the destruction wrought by the Germans in Minsk, Vitebsk, the struggle of the guerrillas. The war has resulted too in a revival of historical painting—a sort of pictorial re-evaluation of Russia's past. Here, Sokolov-Skalya's romanticism has found a fertile source of inspiration.

The war caused a concentration of artistic effort on specific war-time needs, but an intensification of effort has led to the continued expansion of cultural life as a whole. The agenda of the Union of Soviet Artists' five-day plenary session in June, 1943, included a discussion of "Basic problems of Soviet art". In August there was a large exhibition of war posters in Moscow, followed by a three-man show of works by the Kukryniksi. In November at the Tretyakov Galleries there was an exhibition of 600 war paintings. The Museum of the Revolution sent out 140 mobile exhibitions to hospitals, camps and fighting units. The Central and Moscow Houses of Amateur Art arranged a large exhibition entitled "The Great Patriotic War in the Works of its Participants" with paintings and drawings by several hundred Red Army men, guerrillas and workers and collective farmers, members of art clubs and Palaces of Culture. One thousand pictures by amateur artists in the Red Army were exhibited on the occasion of the Red Army's twenty-sixth anniversary. The Committee for Art Affairs took special measures for the development of cultural activities in the newly developing areas of the Urals. This was particularly important during the war years when hundreds of new enterprises were opened there and hundreds of thousands of evacuees arrived. A large number of mobile art exhibitions were sent there, including one devoted to the "Patriotic War" that visited Sverdlovsk, Magnitogorsk and other centres. Thirty leading Soviet artists were commissioned to paint the Ural areas. Additional funds were set aside for the commissioning of work by native artists of the Urals.

There are similar activities in other spheres of art. Thirty-eight thousand new pupils were admitted to music courses in 1943. Six new theatres were opened in the Sverdlovsk (Ural) region alone, and according to the usual practice, one of the metropolitan theatres was assigned to assist the new ventures. In this case it was the Leningrad New Theatre that was trans-ferred *en bloc* to Sverdlov. In the Republics of Central Asia and Transcaucasia alone more than 150 new plays were produced in 1943, including thirty operas. Fifty different languages were used.

July to September, 1943, saw a review of amateur art embrac-ing 10,000 amateur circles. This was organised jointly by the Trades Unions and the local Committees for Art Affairs. Another review of youth amateur art circles covering the whole Union was organised by these bodies and the Young Communist League and Commissariats for Education. During the height of the summer offensive of 1943, eighty concert troupes toured the fronts. The Kazakh section of the Philharmonium (the main concert entertainment organisation) gave 3,000 concerts to farms during the harvest. In October a separate Committee was formed under the Council of Peoples' Commissars with the same status as the Committee for Art Affairs, to supervise and raise the standard of architectural work throughout the Soviet Union with special reference to reconstruction work in the liberated areas.

These facts, taken almost at random from the pages of cultural bulletins, would be impressive in peace-time. In war-time they constitute yet another example of the astounding cultural vitality of the modern Soviet Union.

This virility and vitality in art is an expression of the same forces that have given the Soviet Union the strength and skill and courage to play its present momentous role against Fascism with its obscurantism, spiritual savagery and suppression of culture.

The Soviet Union has shown that planning in the arts does

not mean that a government orders a painter to paint a set number of pictures on a set theme. Soviet planning in the arts is an expression of a new co-operative way of life in which the artists endeavour to plan out their activities on the scale of their state, in the interests of their whole society, just as every artist endeavours to plan his activities to the best advantage on an individual scale. The Soviet artists see no contradiction between their own individual planning and that for the state, for society. The ending of classes, the ending of the possibility of class conflicts within the Soviet state, the identification of individual creative purposes with the larger creative purposes of socialist society are opening out a boundless field for human endeavour and evoking the creative passion to explore and exploit that opportunity to the uttermost. This is the meaning of the October Revolution. This is the source of that vitality of the Soviet arts that have inspired and educated the people for the mighty achievements of peace-time construction and heartened and inspired them to perform unexampled deeds of valour and heroism in the time of the Patriotic War.

CHISWICK PRESS